Louis M. Eilshemius

Songs of Spring and Blossoms of Unrequited Love

Louis M. Eilshemius

Songs of Spring and Blossoms of Unrequited Love

ISBN/EAN: 9783337373689

Printed in Europe, USA, Canada, Australia, Japan

Cover: Foto ©Thomas Meinert / pixelio.de

More available books at **www.hansebooks.com**

SONGS OF SPRING

AND BLOSSOMS OF UNREQUITED LOVE

BY

LOUIS M. ELSHEMUS

Author of "The Moods of a Soul," etc.

Youth's bubbling heart.

WITH 20 ORIGINAL ILLUSTRATIONS BY THE AUTHOR

BUFFALO:
THE PETER PAUL BOOK COMPANY
1895

CONTENTS.

	PAGE.
SPRING	9
WHAT SPRING TELLS ME	10
MYSTERY	13
DIRGE TO DYING MAY	14
THE DIRGE	18
CENTRAL PARK HATH FRESHNESS	20
RHAPSODY	21
LYRICS	29
I LOVE TO CULL THE FLOWERS OF THE DELL	30
COME, SYMPATHIZE WITH ME, O BIRD	31
SONG	32
INVITATION	33
SONG	35
MADRIGAL	36
MORNING-PEARL	37
GOOD-NIGHT	38
A LONGING LOVER'S SONG	40
SORROW IN THE MOUNTAINS	42
AT MIDNIGHT	43
MOMENTARY MEMORIES	44
BY THE FALLS	45
A BUD	46
WHEN LOST IN SCHUMANN'S MUSIC	46
THE LOVED ONE'S IMAGE HAUNTS THE MIND	48
A THRILL	49
COME AGAIN, YOU COMELY, BLISSFUL HOUR	51
LOVE'S DREAM	54
SPRING IS BLUSHING	55

	PAGE.
FLAMES	56
TWO PURPLE VIOLETS I FOUND	56
IN THE DUSK THIS LAY WAS BORN	60
WITH ALL MY HEART I WISHED THAT YOU WERE THERE	62
SHE WAS A NINETEENTH-CENTURY LAMIA	65
A SKETCH FOR HANNAH	67
THE WORKINGS OF THE SOUL	69
DARKNESS GROWS LUMINOUS WHEN THINKING OF THEE	70
IF THE FLOWERS KNEW IT	73
SONG TO MINE ANGELS	74
LOVE'S PUREST JOY	77
O DOVE	78
SUDDEN MUSIC CAME ASTREAMING	79
LOVE'S MOOD	80
SPRING'S VOICELESS RAIN	82
A LOVER'S REQUEST	83
LONELINESS	84
SHE IS FAIREST	85
VAIN WISHES	86
A LIGHTNING-MOMENT OF RAPTURE	87
THE RARE INFLUENCE OF MUSIC	88
MEMORIES, SWEET, YET SORE	92
LOVE'S HISTORY REPEATS ITSELF	93
LOVE IS THE CREATOR	94
SPRING IS HERE	97
MAY-DITTY	100
TO MINE OCARINO	102
A SONG	118
HOPE IS BORN OF CHANGE	119
SPRING-MORNING RHAPSODY	120
THE WHITE VIOLET	124

CONTENTS.

	PAGE.
EVENING-STRAIN	125
THE BLACKBIRD	126
THE SMELL OF SHADE	128
MAY 4TH, 1891	130
PAIN AFTER DREAMS	131
SPRING'S FACILITY TO SING	132
THE WILDERNESS OF MUSIC	133
SING AGAIN	134
IMPROMPTU	135
MAY THE FIRST	136
THIS CAME TO ME	137
NO END	138
NEW BLOOMS	139
CONTENTMENT	140
THREE SPRINGS IN ONE WEEK	141
THE POET	142
NATURE IS NEVER THE SAME	143
TO THE MEADOW-LARK	144
RHAPSODIA	148
AN INSPIRATION	150
RAIN OF SPRING	151
IL PRIMO DI MAGGIO	152
UNO QUESITO	155
ENVOI	157
ERRATA	158

LIST OF ILLUSTRATIONS.

SPRING	Frontispiece
TO TRAIL A WINDING TRUNK TO LANGUID BENDINGS	18
WHERE THE PROCREANT SUN GLINTS THROUGH	30
AS SAD LONG THOUGHTS LIE, SO THE CLOUDS— ABOVE THE HILLS	40
NOR THE FOAM IN THE FLUMES	42
BY THE FALLS	45
IN THE THICKEST DEEPS OF WOODS	55
THEN UP A WINDING ROAD	60
IN THE DUSK THIS LAY WAS BORN	62
A SKETCH FOR HANNAH	67
IN MEASURES—GRACEFUL AS THE THREE!	79
ACROSS THE STRAITS THE MISTY MOUNTAINS LOOM	92
FILL ORCHARDS WITH FRAGRANCE	97
WHERE SALMACIS YET DWELLED ALONE	103
WHERE THE DRAGON-FLIES FEED UPON THE TALL WHITE LILIES	111
THE MARINERS THE FIFES OF GHOST-WINDS HEAR!	113
FOR CLOUDS WERE HANGING O'ER THE SKY	119
THE STONY BROOKLET'S PET	124
AWAY FROM DIMPLING DALES	136
SBALZA LA CAPRICUOLA	153

SONGS OF SPRING

SPRING.

NOW Spring, with flowery fillets, dances through the East !
 On snow-drop, bee, dove, asp, and roaming beast,
She breathes a vital spell—blushes to trees, brooks, meads ;
 O'er nature gently sways her magic wand—
 From highest peak, to glistening, sea-laved strand.
Then smiles in transport ; then her beaming eye-flash leads
 Her morris-step to man—oh ! ecstasy—
His soul she lulls to love, new-born of Heaven's Glee !

WHAT SPRING TELLS ME.

"COME, O beauty-bathéd Spring!
    Tell me all you have in store,
    On your flower-walled arbor-floor;
Tell me, maiden-minded Spring!"
"I am bashful all to tell;—
There are snow-drops for the dell,
But a red runs o'er my cheek
When I of the roses speak:
For they tint the soft, blithe loves,
Sighing, smiling in ash groves.
Carols of the birds I tune,
Till they warbling sound in June.
Look not at me now—I blush—
By my touch those roses flush!
Yonder nook grows suckle sweet—
Bees press on them with their feet.
Now, look through that jessamine bush,—
Listen to what I tell thee—push
All those yellow sweets away—
They are waiting for the May!
I sprinkle airs with golden rain—
Flowers that look like harvest-grain!
Flushed am I, mine eyes seem joy—
I feel more like a flippant boy!

For I send to hearts and minds
Sweetly-scented, dreamy winds :
They swing joyfully o'er streams ;
Fill the mounts with Magyar-dreams ;
Listen on hoary darkling pines,
Sigh on billows ;—sweep o'er shrines
(Where Love wafts his incense-fumes.)
Laugh o'er cypress-lulled tombs ;
Dash adown a glow-abyss ;
Fervently dove-nature kiss.
Step not on those trailing vines !
See: white flowers with pinkish lines ;
Find them in the moist rich woods,
Hiding, where the small snake broods.
Ay, redberries !—taste their flavor !
Like the cherry's is their savor . . .
Laugh away—"

" Ay, my bonnie lassie, Spring !
How may'st thou tell all to me—
Arbor thine is vast as sea—
Ay, my languid beauty, Spring ! "

" My dowers are many
As winds that thrid through crook and cranny ;
Come ! let's dance around together !—
Yea, I fill with wine the weather :
With love's vintage, Heaven-thrilled ;
In drifting globes of Truth, distilled ;

Strained then by coy Purity;
Quaffed in lands where God's love be!
Ay, I would not tell thee all
I let on earth's people fall:
Mostly, Love revivified—
This is not to one denied!
Then I color fields with flowers;
Then I send sweet cooling showers;
I fill the walks with songs; the trees,
Through whose twigs flow prophecies,
I deck with juicy vestments green;
The groves I trim—the grotts are sheen:
Beetles burn in armors bright;
Fishlings dazzle in charmed light!
Cliffs I sash with red glow-bands;
Rocks are green with moss-coats; sands
Thrill with flies—that glimmer in sun—
To renew man's love 'tis done!
For he then may roam o'er fields;
Lip the honey, clover yields:
Drink the cooling water—lie
Down in thought, muse 'neath the sky.
Love may bloom but in my bower—
Love and I burst from one flower.
Lovers want so many things,
   They are never satisfied—
Yet I bring new marvellings—
   So give all—to none denied!"

"Thanks, thanks! O beauty-bathéd Spring!
  Each man may see thy bounteous dowers,
  Sweet-falling like some heaven-sprinkled showers,
Thanks, thanks! O maiden-minded Spring!

"For the sake of Love thou givest—
For Love's growth thou ever livest—
Each may cull some dower to his choice—
Thou, Spring! knowest he will aye rejoice!

"Thanks, O lovely-minded Spring!
  Thou hast shown me all thy dowers;
  Love may cull the choicest flowers!
Thanks, Love-lulling and Love-breeding Spring!!"
1885

MYSTERY.

O THE mystery of things!
  Scarce, from its downy nest,
  The bluebird beauteously sings—
  Then falls to sudden rest!

O the mystery of thought!
  When void stares o'er the eyes—
  What wonders hours have wrought:
  That sing of songful skies!

DIRGE TO DYING MAY.

A train of mourners walk aslowly;
Weird drums and fifes a dead-march play;
Its harmony alike to this hath flowing:

REVERBERATIONS of the roaring river
   Are carried, by the thundering wind,
     To nooks in woods, where faintly they do sound;
And there they sweetly echoed are forever
By all the feathered warblers in the round;
And each hath chosen a lay to his own mind.
And the full-toned sway of the foaming stream
Is born anew to one harmonious woodland-dream!

Autumn lunges loudly into Summer's bloom!
And whirls the wiltering wood-leaves in his wrath;
Till sear they lie; and snow turns them to earth—
While Winter sheds his shroud o'er Nature's tomb;—
They feed the trees at future welcome birth,
When Spring strews flowers o'er all the forest-path,—
And the mouldered leaves that lie in the woods
Give rich food for the newly-greening solitudes!

Moulds may not perish on this living sphere!
In them a vital flood bounds on—for aye!

Dirge to Dying May. 15

A witching warble mates the woodbird wild—
Sweet passion pelts a soothing shower o'er deer
And doe;—sweet coaxing lisps, till whispers mild
Unite the breeze with calm repose of day!
And the love, that is in woman and man,
Will ever see fresh minds spring up in life's bold van!

The train's wild tones are hushed, like to a sigh.
The drums are still—the fifes no longer play.
They all stop by a fragrant woodland-way. . . .
When all are mourning in the grasses high,
A virgin chanteth, to a wildly-wielded harp, a sweet sad
    lay:

On the last day of the blossomiest month of the
    years
We mourn;—and shed some silent tears!
Away are the blossoms on boughs of briery trees—
Only moans through their twigs a mourning breeze;
Then wails in agony, and moans—and moans—and
    moans:
Now despairingly, then faints in sighing undertones!

May, sweetest month of the long, long year,
Is resting peacefully in her violet-bier.
Nor shall her tender cheeks all bloom again
Till eleven long months will lave the changeful plain!
And a sigh for her—fairest!
And a tear for her—dearest!

With a sparkle of hope in our eye—
Like the sorrel-gleam in the gloomy sky!

Strew delicate violets, that grow alone—
Sweet-scented, and white, by a shady stone.
Her grave the loud wind wardeth;
The coming balmly weather guardeth!
The aspen shall bloom where she lieth—
By the wood, where the runnel plieth!

For the last day of the sweetest month of the year
We mourn! and shed a silent tear!
Away are the blossoms, the fragrant blooms away—
And no dear word to ask mild May to stay!

O May is dead! Her bloom is in a violet-bier—
The train mourn through the sorrowing forest-lanes.
And while they walk all slowly—
A cymbal-cadence clashes loudly through the train:

If May be dead, with her petals on the mead!
Her petals O rosy, white, and odorous and fair—
She dieth for a greater bloom, when all the air
Is redolent with shining fruits, and golden seed!

A trailing wind-breath stops the passing train—
And clutcheth May's sweet violet-bier;—
With scents and rich perfumes He soars away again
And this the wondering train do hear:

Dirge to Dying May.

No grave be dug for May—melliferous May!
Her sweetest robe may fade, and brown the way—
But all her fragrance, the rich exuberance
Of her coy breath—her charming, melting glance—
They wed my gaze, while through the dreary last May-day
Her charms I carry on to lands, with many a bay
To freshen all their maiden-bloom through the long year.
There blow I blandly; soften all their spirit-gear;
Till, when fleet Time hath left his icy cave
I bring May back, and let her all your woodlands lave.
O May may not lie in a cold, dark grave;
Nor sit, like a voiceless stone, in a damp, large tomb.
There is a shore where an ever calm-swung wave
Laps the green lea—May sleeps there, as at home!

And ere the train acclaim could raise,
Or give to Wind their one-tongued praise—
Oh! far they heard the whispering in the wet-leaved trees—
And May was gone—and all her blossoming did cease!
Then, like a mist-band (pendant o'er some rocky path),
That, when the loud wind shouteth out his wilful wrath,
Ascends the peak—then vanishes in lofty air—so they,
The stounding train, were swept by mystic influence away!
They were not clay, nor bred with our so cumbrous blood—
Quick spirits they, that dwell now by some reedy flood,
Then lively fly to regions where no lambkins play.

THE DIRGE.

AY, are the blossoms gone, all nipped by tempest's lip!
    The blossoms of the May! whom beelings sought, to sip
Their nectarine wine; and birds had piped in vine-run briers,
To quaff their quaint perfume, like strains from lulling lyres!

Gone the rank sprays of wild choke cherries, whose wild scent
Calls up voluptuous scenes in some high sultan's tent:
With their white limbs, and breasts atremble to the flow
Of musk-wooed essense—and the bliss of passion's woe!

Where the long, juicy grass is blue, I loved to lull my thought;
To trail a winding trunk to languid bendings, that were wrought
With dear intent; then peer at the rich green, and rosy bloom
Of myriad blossoms! oh! and are they flown—the green is gloom?

TO TRAIL A WINDING TRUNK TO LANGUID BENDINGS . . . .   Page 18.

The Dirge.

On my lone walks, the orchards were a calm delight,
But since the thunder clashed, purple flashes filled the night!
And streaming rain had lashed the herbs, and ploughed the roads—
My eyes were sad—I saw no more those bunchy loads!

Ay, have they left the green and blue-brown hillside lone!
Those patches here and there of snow!—the catkins gone?
That flaked the breezy noon, and sailed their spokéd wool
From willow to hazel, from rushings to the sorrel-pool!

Ay, are they gone, those roséd blossoms, all those tender buds!
All sweetest musings swept with their pinked, fragrant petal-floods!
Bland thoughts with them are flown; the loving eye longs for a spray!
Ay, blossoms gone! and dead is May!—ay, past is scented May!

ITHACA, N. Y., 1886.

CENTRAL PARK HATH FRESHNESS.

'TIS heavenly dear, to leave the city's sound—
Where Vice and Crime conspire to fade the
bloom—
To stray at some feet from it, where the boom
Is silenced! Where a saner stream flows round,
As though peer-Purity had wreathings wound
In all the air! As if she sprent neat broom
Pervading the chill park with staid perfume,
That clung to sear grass on the frosty ground!

There whispered one lone breath of Spring! the sky
Was clear, and freshly fluted the bare wood.
A stillness reigned;—then tender symphony
From unseen angels cheered the solitude—
Unbroken—save the peacock's shrilly cry;
Or wheel's low sound in shady neighborhood!

RHAPSODY.

YOUTH.

O TIME ! bring back my wild, wild childhood ;
When the days seemed filled with fairy-
dreams !
My heart was then deep in the wild-wood ;
And my thoughts would catch all sunny beams !

TIME.

Never, never may those days live fresh again !
Thy days, with the butterfly-hours.
Thine eves, with the joyous voice.
Thy morns, with the lark-like showers.
Thy noons, with the brooklet-noise !
Never, never ! Youth ! thy childhood's gone—and
vain

Thy pleadings to the votary of Life.
I, fleet-footed, light-hearted, tarry never.
I travel onward, o'er this globe, forever.
The days that are flown—are flown like the mist,
That whitens, then glimmers like faint amethyst,
Then dies—like the memory of Strife !

MANHOOD.

Time! sweetest friend to Knowledge, studious mornings;
Waft one dear hour, when my first love was all!
When days seemed ages, blossomed with Love's adornings.
Give back my youth, O Love's own thrall!
Let the passion-flower, that hangs so lovely, down yon arbor's vault,
Spell one sweet day, when lips said words that now my thoughts exalt!

TIME.

Never, never may those days bloom rosy-flushed!
 Thy days, with the longing hours.
  Thy nights, with trysts, and kisses bland.
 Thy lark-morns, with her purple flowers.
  Those long-shadowed groves—with her magic hand!
Never, never! Man—thy sweet love wanes—is hushed,

 By the sterner sentiment that swells in thee.
World's days are born—till this sod will be green!
And I, ever roving, will be master! and sheen
The moments ever brighter—but never shall call
Those younger morns again! and in that Hall
 My fleet hours will melt in calm Eternity!

AGE.

Oh ! if the burthen of years be still oppressive
    weight—
And if my days are weary of the same-sung
    life—
Ay, Time ! then pass those days when I was strong
    and great,
Before my sleepful mind, or guide me back to
    strife,
To Fame, Ambition—to those thundering echoes
    loud
That made my Glory worthy—all my pulses proud !

TIME.

Never, never, snow-flecked head, those days will
    come !
Thy days, with the eager heart aft' fame,
Thine arbor-hours, all culling laurels won.
Thy pensive hours, that bloomed a world-known
    name ;
Thy luck-lulled evens—all when her fair eyes
    shone !
Never, never, ashen locks, will those hours bloom !
I am the magic ceaseless waterfall !
Whose waters bound from fathomless and living
    Springs,
Way far in mist-hung wolds of Past ! and roar
    adown,

With wondrous waywardness, the Cliff of Life
    that rings
  From faint and sullen-whispering drops, that
    stopped for call
Of lichens, crouching in the ruts and darker
    holes !
  No air-swung drop is stayed ! each foaming
    crown
Of white succeeds its swathing precedent—nor
    stops
To dally on a fern's small bud ; but from the tops
  Of jutting rocks, they tumble rapidly, till all
    The drops, the spray, the foam, and these com-
      mingled, fall
Into that calm, blue sea of ever cooled souls !
  I am that magic, ceaseless waterfall !
  Whose great volume never wooes the western
    wind ;
Never weds a main, whose bosom's kissed by a wan
    moon !
But whose ever-freshened fluid flows from noon to
    noon—
  Uninfected—pure, not tracing foam behind !
  I am that magic, ceaseless waterfall !

AGE.

Oh ! then plunge me deep into that deep blue sea !
Calm, deep sea : Eternity !

Rhapsody.

Where the moments, hours, years,
Aeons of these seething Sneers,
Mingle, link—and flow in love
To those marvel-halls above !
Time ! then drag me with thy sway
From these Rocks and Caves away !
Till the foam be calmed to waves—
Till their Calm that Joy-Shore laves,
Where, in fragrant Temples, dwells
He, who there our Mystery tells!
Time! then plunge me deep into that calm, deep
    sea :
Deep, blue sea : Eternity !
　　WILLIAM'S FARM, ITHACA, N. Y.

BLOSSOMS OF UNREQUITED LOVE
TO A. L. H.—1885-90.

LYRICS.

OH! the sweet balm to a life unwedded—
When all hours useless seem—
Lyrics are the strokes of fingers
On life's lyre—fair as dream!

Ah! the hope-fire of a life unwedded
When all days so dreary are—
Lyrics seem the pulses throbbing;
Sure of better life afar!

Lyrics are the only solace, sweetning
Unrequited love's sad hours—
Were no lyrics known to mortals,
We'd be slain by sorrow's powers!

I LOVE TO CULL THE FLOWERS OF THE DELL.

I LOVE to cull the flowers of the dell:
  The golden bloom; the teeming asphodel;
  The sweet star-seer; the anemones;
The violets, by roots of mossed oak-trees;
Their staid white sisters, where the glassy pool
Reflects the sailing clouds and Spring's light blue;
The soft arbutus, where the shade is cool;
The trillium, where the procreant sun glints
    through.

I love to cull the flowers of the dell.
For think I then to be a maiden sweet;
A maiden pure as is the asphodel,
And modest as the blushing marguereet.
And while I stoop for all the sweetest blooms
I think I kneel before some angels rare.
And oh! they tell me beauteous tales, so fair—
Of fragrant gardens and of flower-made rooms;
And joys such that the whispering lovers share,
When balmy blows June's wanton, vagrant air.

Oh! then I well would wish to be a maid,
And be, as is the asphodel, so staid.

WHERE THE PROCREANT SUN GLINTS THROUGH....
Page 30.

For woe could not be mine, nor tears, nor pain—
But flower-dreams, and flower-dreams again!
WHITE MTS., N. H., 1886.

COME, SYMPATHIZE WITH ME, O BIRD!

COME, swift-flying bird of Spring!
   Come! and flit about my head—
Carol to the greedy world
   That I am dead!
For evening seems the glorious morn—
Eve howleth as a dark storm-sea;
And night hath no more golden stars—
So lilt: my love hath left me lorn!
Spring's fructifying heat seems cool—
The willow seems a haunting ghoul.
All cries: oh! how forlorn is he!
And each sweet sound my heart-throb mars.

O come, Spring's prettiest musician—
You may revive my clay's attrition.
Come, perch upon my locks, and sing,
That I am dead, that I am dead;
And flit thou round my drear-grown head.
And sing to all the world this ditty:
"*To him who dies in longing: pity!*
For he had deep, deep sorrowing!"

SONG.

My Love! it is raining;
    Pray, stay on the porch.
  For the clouds are complaining,
    They drench Cupid's torch!
Pray stay! lest thy mab-feet be wet in the spray
Of rain, and thou shiverest all through the day!

  O linger; and listen—
    In the ivied low porch—
  Till the large rain-drops glisten—
    And wet Cupid's torch.
Ay, listen to the patter and tinkle in the leaves!
To birds piping loudly, and thronging the eaves!

  O dream there alone
    Where the rain cometh not!
  Of melodies gone
    That tranced our thought.
Ay sitting where ivy low dangles and greens;
Ay, dreaming of love in thine innocent teens!

  My flower, 'tis raining.
    Pray, stay on the porch!
  The rain will be waning,
    Till glows Cupid's torch!

And while thou art musing and humming a strain,
Let Love's hours be blooming thy dreaming again !

    Love! stay there, and listen !
      Soon all will be glee,
      The snow-clouds will glisten
      For the birds' jubilee !
When looking at dancing of drops in the pool,
Let love-thoughts awake for thine own little fool !

INVITATION.

MY sweetest soul—mine own true Annie,
    Come walk in the garden with me !
  For the shower is over, the clouds are fleeing,
    And the freshness thrills;—see, see:
How the trees are burge'ning; the grass is greening;
    The birds sing sweet minstrelsy !

Oh ! walk beside me, thy hand upon my shoulder,
    Thy lips parted, prattling lover's lays.
For the vernal shower hath gladdened the thrilling
      bird-songs,
    And gilded the bushes' bell-flowered sprays;
Hath budded the maples—hath tasselled the lindens
      and willows;
    And cooled all the green-fringed forests and ways!

Come Annie, mine only sweetest soul in blossom!
  Come, feel the pulsings of spring-shed showers!
A sweeter breath is wafted—the air is cooler—
  An inspiring thrill revives our powers!
For the rain that poured through the morning was
    of Springtime;
  Had an essense that unfolded the flowers.

Come Annie! hasten with me to the garden's corner,
  Where the morn has opened a pale pink bud:
On a bush, with netted leaves, and smell its perfume:
  A fresh Spring-scent, yet bearing a flood
Of a deathly odor, like the tuberose's—
  Though it still had Winter's paly blood!

My sweetest soul, mine own dear loving Annie;
  Enraptured, gaze into mine eye!
For the fresh sweet air is bathing us, cool as water—
  And the blushing treebuds prophesy
That our love will, one day, be fresh, and sweet and
    blooming
  Like Spring-shower's emotive melody!

Annie, hasten to the joy-breathing garden!
  Where maid-Spring hath wept her tears—
With a soul that's mine—a heart that's beating
  To be mine for many years!
For the rain is over—the grass is brighter—
  And young nature lavishes cheers!
    BROOKLYN, L. I.

SONG.

COME to the Spring-greened lawn—
　　Where some trees are in leaf.
　All in the cool-breathed dawn,
　　Exalt love—and kill grief !

See ! jewelled grass-blades glisten,
　　In such dappled star-light.
Hark !—to the gay birds, listen !
　　They shake songs with delight!

Tears of the night are gemmed
　　To fair diamonds at morn !
Woe is bright diademmed
　　When a hope-dream is born !

Come to the glittering green,
　　It is morn, mine own love !
All the smile-lawn's in sheen—
　　By warm sun-rays above !

MADRIGAL.

AY, tuck thy silken stole,
    For the vernal shower is now descending.
The first loud thunderings roll ;
And the purple levin my sight is blending.
    Flashes the lightning, with a purple light,
                                  A flight.
    Clashes the thunder, with a lion's roars,
                               Out of doors !

    Ay, come, Love, under shelter !
For the drops are digging holes in the ground.
    All nature's in helter-skelter !
For louder is the thunder's sound.
The levin is gilt—then is whitened—and is
    hurried. . . .
                          Be not worried !
Clashes come after—then roll, then are fainting—
    dying—
                Like sea-waves' sighing !

    It is the first Spring-shower
Of the year, when the clouds rehearse their voice—
    Regain their canon's power
To be booming their Summer's deafning noise.
All the rain-drops grow to fluid balls, that slash,
                            And plash.—

All the rain-rune wearies to a monotone—
    A tinkling on a stone !

O Love ! now brighten thy face !
For the levin lights not, nor the clashes are calling.
    Be hardy in thy grace !
For the drops in their sing-song now are falling.
All the sweet spatter on stones will soon be a play—
    Of some hours away !
Arm in arm, soon we two may be sipping the air,
    By thee made sng fair !

MORNING-PEARL.

ARISE, o sweetest pearl, arise !
    For the sweet smell of morn is spent—
    Aurora blushes; Venus flies !
Hyperion for his steeds hath sent,
And the golden chariot he mounts:
To leave his gilt castle and midnight founts;
Then gallop his neighing steeds
On the road that to dark Leto's chamber leads.
    Arise, o sweetest pearl, arise!
For the cold spectres of night are flown.
    Fair Flora breathes, where Darkness sighs !
In the air morn's pure perfumes are blown.

Arise, Arise !
'Tis Phoebus glows. See the blushing skies !
Arise, Arise !
O sweetest pearl, arise !

GOOD-NIGHT !

GOOD-NIGHT ! mine only love, good-night !
Oh ! let thy lids lie on thy sparkling pupil's bay!
Thy dainty hands enfold; thy purest prayer
    pray !
Then think of me, and, in thy orison's wreath,
Let memory exhale one loving breath !
Then rest in calm, and holy peace !
My love, then let thy heart-throbs cease.
Good-night ! mine only love, good-night !

   * * * * *

See Nox, dark daughter of Chaos, blackest of moulds,
 Hath stayed her two cimmerian mares !
  They drink at the golden horn;
While Erebus, hoar, ebon-faced, her infants holds:
 One to ethereal lispings born,
 And one the light of day so fondly wears!
She who may wax in seven causes great
 And wane from all, till she doth live as Night--

Good-Night.

Hath retinue so golden—for her they wait—
While the mares snort—breathe a milky breath of
  light,
That flows along the heaven's vaulted halls!
Then rolls the chariot onward—with stars escorting,
Through the darkness;—there a small star falls!
And cuts a path—and eats a cave in the dark earth.—
While above the ebon mares are wildly snorting,
The gold-throng sing to Nox her darkly worth!
*   *   *   *   *

Mine only love ! the bats have gone to bed !
  The owls are not hooting in affright.
But the full-moon is golden, the stars are red—
  The mabs are revelling in charmed delight !
Then sleep ! mine only sweet—my dear !
The night is dark, and dank, and drear !
Cover thy lily-bosom—thy dainty small feet
With the snow-white sheet !
So scented with sweets—to dream me asleep !
O happy those Angels who for thee fond vigils
  keep !

Good-night ! mine only love, good-night !
Coy Purity sleeps neath thy pillow—O, so soft;
  Beneath the sheets sweet Chastity lies lowly;
Thy dreams are born of purest thought O, way aloft!
  Thy face is placid—like a nun's, so holy.
    Good-night ! mine only love, good-night !
Sleep sound ! sweet maid, sleep peacefully !

The roses, that clamber about the low wall,
Waft all their opiate fumes for thee!
  Ay, soon the fresh morn with his clear horn will call !—
  Good-night, O sweetest love ! Good-night !
BROOKLYN, L. I., 1886.

A LONGING LOVER'S SONG.

ONE eastern star sighs on the pine
    Darkning with one black mountain-range;
  It twinkles through the ebon crest,
    Then leaves this vale, so weird and strange:
Oh ! strange, that Annie breathes no rose-like breath—
Oh ! weird, for no small brook her sweet name saith!

The sickle-moon so brightly shines,
    Her friendly star, as constant mate—
Her saffron stole is swathed with fumes
    Of jassmines—while the eve grows late.
But no fond dove to whisper me love's tale;—
And chilled my blood—my cheeks so pale, so pale!

As sad, long thoughts lie, so the clouds
    Above the hills, so black as they,
Burthened with tears of days ago—
    As is my mind with love's dismay.

AS SAD LONG THOUGHTS LIE, SO THE CLOUDS—ABOVE THE HILLS.
Page 40.

A Longing Lover's Song.

O Anne, how darkling grows my loving mood:
To pine, and wail in mockèd solitude !

There trailed passed me a woman fair;
  She seemed like Anne, mine own true love.
How brightest moments burst in me!
  Each feature sang of Anne, my love!
And Anne was in the moon, and in the wold—
And in the stars, and where the brook is gold!

What may befall thy lover true,
  If never thy fond face he sees.
Come soon! To gladden his lonely hours,
  Ere sound Death's hallowed symphonies!
For he is longing—he is woe-begone,
He'll die, if he must breathe his days alone!

Eve kisses night! 'Tis drear and dark!
  Oh! there the rich-gold, ringlet-moon
Sinks down.—A mystery it leaves
  On my sick heart: for late, or soon
O Anne! thou must be mine, O Heaven's Anne!
O Anne, we must be one! oh! Angel-Anne!
  JACKSON, WHITE MOUNTAINS, N. H.

SORROW IN THE MOUNTAINS.

DEEP in the heart of the mountains
    My tears flow bitterly.
  Far from my sweetest own loved-one,
    My heart bleeds fast and free!
But the watery wind may not drench my woe,
Nor the trembling falls in their silvery flow!

  Deep in the depth of the cañons
    My heart yearns for my dove.
  Way in the groves of the valleys
    My whispers breathe: Oh! love!
But the purl of the founts may not soothe my loss;
Nor the foam in the flumes that the storm-winds
    toss!

CRAWFORD NOTCH, WHITE MOUNTAINS, N. H.

NOR THE FOAM IN THE FLUMES . . . .

AT MIDNIGHT.

ONLY patters thickly the large-dropped rain—
While the dark is uncanny to see!
Drear, soft splashes pass the window-pain—
Only mutter the drops their sobs again—
While the dark is uncanny to see!
Weirdly drip chilled waters to the lane—
    Alone in the chamber am I
    And weep, and cry!
    For far is mine Annie, my love;
    My bliss—my dove!

Only sounds so hollow the drippling shower—
While the pines seem like phantoms so tall!
Low the plash sounds through the midnight-hour—
Wet hang vines—soaked cold the arbor-flower—
While the large drops of heaven-tears fall!
Only splash the drops—low murmurs cower—
    Asad in the loneliness I
    But weep—and sigh—
    For far is mine Annie, my heart—
    My life—my smart!
CRAWFORD NOTCH, WHITE MTS., N. H.

MOMENTARY MEMORIES.

OH! those half-hour chats, oh! those half-hour smiles;
  Oh those half-hour communions with thee, dear Anne!
Like the budding return of the spring-born wiles
  In the bobolink's voice, so they soothe me, Anne!

From here, where I'm lonely on the bank of the brook,
  That gurgles o'er there—here it soundeth like wind!
I see the bright image-filled clouds from this nook,
The blossoming boughs—and the bare oaken rind;
  And list to the dreams of the twittering merl;
    While near me the waters their fleeting waves curl.
And here, where I'm lonely, and longing for thee—
  Those words from thy lips, when we shared what love yields,
Are borne by the wind, that is shaking the tree—
  Alas! to be scattered all over the fields!

* * * * *

Oh! those half-hour days, when our love was young—
  Oh, those half-hour songs, that have thrilled my heart—

BY THE FALLS.

By the Falls.

They are back in my mind, while the clouds, low-
 hung,
Fashion visions, to soothe my deep longing's
 smart !
ENDFIELD BROOK, ITHACA, N. Y.

BY THE FALLS.

RUSH ! yon fall of liquid snow !
 Rush ! with low, low thunder-tone !
Sound as storms that lash sea-foam;
As wind through oaks, grown long ago !
Splash your feet on the deep green pool;
Murmur with inner-voice, as lispings gone
Of her, who pineth in her golden home;
Who spelled my soul those last days at the school !
The sun is kissing all your white silk-bredes;
Afar the meadow-lark sings in the meads.
Your gloomy-caves are lit by hanging ferns;
You murmur as men speak, when all alone !
O Fall ! you haunt me, and your cooling flow !
But her sweet lucid throat, whose breath
Is violet-scent—it is not here;
Her languid laugh, her glance, are gone:
O glance that thrilled me two long sorrow-weeks
 ago !

And Fall, oh! whose great tumult "glory!" saith,
Though freshness flows, you seem so drear—
For my love-lip for her rose-dimple yearns!
   ENDFIELD BROOK, ITHACA, N. Y.

A BUD.

OUR love is like a bud, so rosy-blown—
   It waits till June her blessings will have strown
   To bloom it, fit for Cleopatra's throne!

WHEN LOST IN SCHUMANN'S MUSIC.

OH! why were the strings sounding fuller and
     fresher than e'er,
   Like cool wind that's blown o'er some morn-
   ing-kissed sea to the shore!
Were thoughts of her wafted to me, from the one I
     adore—
Were perfumes of richest flushed flowers sweet-
     scenting the air,

While flowed, as Aeolian flutings, the Romanza so
 fair!
While mellowed sweet harmonies colored the strain
 evermore;
And ripplings, like love-runing rills, trebled trill'r-
 ingly o'er.
Oh! why were the strings sounding cheery, and
 clary and fair!

A fairy hath flown to me, messaging me my love's
 dream!
 In spirit she sipped some hoar sorcerer's magic-
 made wine—
O'er odorous orchards she soared till there flashed
 a fair beam:
 A torch for a way to my soul!—Oh! I now may
 divine
Why sounded the strings so intensely as Seraph's
 own theme—
*Her thoughts, that I heard not, were gloriously
 havened in mine!*
 LONG ISLAND, N.Y.

THE LOVED ONE'S IMAGE HAUNTS THE MIND.

OH ! in my room's obscurity,
   I saw a gliding apparition gleam !
   My eyes were open, it was no dream—
As she, it moved so maidenly !

It moved with step so slow and proud—
   Like a pale-purple cloud at evening's close—
   So silently, as waftings from a rose
That blooms in dew-swathed gloaming's shroud !

It seemed like her, I see at day !
   But her bright eyes were cold—her auburn hair
   Dishevelled—her lips were veiled with whiteness rare !
Her speech was gone—her bloom away !

So stately moved it, as a swan
   That glides o'er tranquil moonlit lake, and sings;
   Oh ! sings a languid song, and flaps its wings:
To breathe the balm of higher dawn !

It moved before me through the gloom. . .
But when my supplicating arms were raised,
Her maiden-phantom vanished !—All amazed,
I wondered in my sweetened room !
LONG ISLAND, N. Y.

A THRILL.

OH! it may never leave me
    That happy, blesséd day—
    There's not an earthly flower
       That glows like its array !
North, West, South, East—their dowers;
    The rosy flush of virgin-dawn,
The breath of fairy-hours;
    The mad-kiss on a crocus-lawn;
Are cresses to its beauteous bloom—
May not its glorious glow assume!
Oh! on that blesséd morning,
    Mine eyes saw languishment
Of love's frame, O so lovely.
    It wafted love's own scent.
It seemed dissolving slowly
As vision, seraphs sing to,
That smiles, and beckons to you;

Then faints,—the vision never
May leave your haunted soul—
It haunts like vernal forest-toll!
Oh! it may leave me never
No image blooms here, on this globe,
To semble its quaint longing.
High Heaven's host may sing, and robe
It saintly—but the fragrance
Is wafted but to one
Who saw—to him alone!
Those eyes—that head so dreaming—
That brow, as Heaven wished to bend—and kiss!
That body, longing me to fondle—
Oh! languid all, all lost in over-bliss!
Oh! it may never leave me
   That languid, piercing glance!
Oh! then she surely loved me,
   Languished in lover's trance!
   LONG ISLAND, N. Y.

"COME AGAIN, YOU COMELY, BLISSFUL HOURS!"

COME again, you comely, blissful hours!
    When *one* glance had burst our hearts!
    Come! with fuller bloom, more love-filled
      showers;
    Come! with Cupid's roséd darts!

Beauty bunches roses: red, saffron, and pale—
    Truth attends to blossoms white, and myrtles
      green—
Let both Truth and Beauty sprinkle her wedding-
      veil—
    With their flowers fair, she'll glow an elfin-queen!
Crimsoned Levant hath stolen all those hours—
    For when she passed, my thoughts were thrilled!
All ponent breezes wafted them in showers:
    The rain was with their perfumes filled!
Rosy East!—O West! that glowest fire-flamed!
    Bring to me again those blissful hours!

To my thoughts bring back those comely hours!
Waft their lovelinesses in spring-sweetened showers!
Bring to me their fragrance, tenfold sweeter—
    Till, when Eros hath our love-day named—

Flow the perfume more than sweetly; let our thoughts be fleeter!
Bring to me again those blissful hours:
Waft their lovelinesses in spring-sweetened showers!

   * * * * *

The shallop of scented sweetness hath stored them
In the hulk, hewn of Ind's purest poom-wood.
She sails, when morn's pink's aglow—morn's star pales;
When thrushes outtune the sweet nightingales!
Full swollen by a breeze that Love's pure lips blow
Sailing, to far days that live in Love's glow! . .
Those hours—how my dreamy thoughts have adored them!
When gloamed the fair eve—when upstarted my gloom-mood!
That shallop, she glideth o'er the sea's bosom:
So calm—save a ripple there, the sea's blossom!
She sails to a far sweet Mango-girt haven;
To a gold-bosomed, orange-glistening harbor.
Then those hours shall hie o'er streets, vermeil-paven—
To a large-blossomed rose-bush arbor!
Ay, hours! stay there, 'mong blossoms full red—
Stay there, till her eyes Love's message have said!

The soul is sweet—the mind moves on—
The heart is precious—blood is boon—

"Come Again, You Comely, Blissful Hours." 53

Her soul and mind are mine alone—
Her heart and blood pulse like to mine;—
Those hours fair shall pulse and throb asoon
Again—our lips speak words divine!
Come back again, you comely, blissful hours—
When Joyance 'tween our heart-throbs flowed—
Come, sheen again! like sun-lit vernal showers.
Let Flora fly with lovely flower-load!

* * * * *

Oh! live again! ere the crocus cuts the mouldered leaves—
Ere ponds reflect the full-pink-blossomed young peach trees!
Oh! shout again! ere the ocean's warm, ere the wold-air heaves
In glistening glare! Oh! come ere Hymen hums, at ease,
His voluptuous ditties to the June-enamored breeze!
Envelope all your thoughts with azaleas' blood-red bloom;
Young hyacinths; odorous heliotropes, and sweetest broom;
Narcissi, valley-lilies, lilacs white, and pinks!
Bathe in a crystal lake, where oft the white doe drinks;

Till fresh you bloom, like fragrant shower-bathéd air,
That maketh Ramapura's groves glow more than fair!
Then sprinkle the drops from off your honeyed tresses
On our young souls—and bid that Love us blesses!
APRIL, LONG ISLAND, N. Y.

LOVE'S DREAM.

MY love is like the holy angel
    That listeneth to the heavenly tones!
My love is like the seraph-singing
When all Elysium teems with thrones!
And though on these cold rocks I may not kiss her brow—
Oh! there! in cooling blowings will she breathe her vow!

My love is fairer than the flower
    That bends to drink from woodland-pool;
My love is fresher than the shower
    That springs from violet-dales so cool!

IN THE THICKEST DEEPS OF WOODS . . . .

Page 55.

My love is far too good and tender for this earth.
Oh! how our souls will be together—at higher
    birth!
LONG ISLAND N. Y.

SPRING IS BLUSHING.

OH! Spring is blushing—
    From the glowing hills
  The boiling torrents are rushing—
And beauty fills
  The scene, and prospect far!

Oh! Spring is blooming—
In the thickest deeps
  Of woods the cascades are booming—
And gladness peeps
  From earth—from evening's star!

Oh! Spring is telling
How all is loving, loving—
  How heart's Love-fountains are welling,
How lovers are roving
  With bonny lassies through brake, o'er plain!

Yet low, in the nooks of my heart,
    Like the sonorous thuds of the waterfall,
There are moans, like drear ululation-sound!
For my smart—
My Love-inflicted wound,
    Is cold—then doth appall!
    And it burns—is cold—then bursts to pain!
LONG ISLAND, N. Y.

FLAMES.

LOVE'S eternal fire that burns in my torn heart
    Is like drear Ætna's—it will never part!

"TWO PURPLE VIOLETS I FOUND."

TWO purple violets I found—
    At the dreamy bourne of the dun-stoled brake:
    Where all the sear leaf-covered ground
Drank the shower's wine, for sweet Spring's own
    sake!

When the gloaming had gloomed the glowing West!
And the violets were nodding their heads to rest!

   Two violets I plucked alone!
No sweet scent they had, but a thought of thee
   Fond gave to them a myrrh-breath—won
By the memory of days that have smiled for me.
And their purple perfume brought back the breath
That the air loves, when thy voice murmureth!

   With thoughts of thee, my Love, I glanced
At the moon, oh! ambered by the sun's last kiss!
   But half on her queen-course advanced:
Oh! a hope: the goal may be crowned by Love's bliss!
Now she glowed!—then brown films did fret the gold—
Again queen: sweet she dreamed of ages old!

   With violets, close to my cheek—
While the rustling leaves startled the late blue-bird,
   That awing, beat its bonnie beak
To soft trills: so dear, when the South-breeze stirred!
And I thought of thee, love! gay singing here—
But the gloom of the eve shed saddest tear!

   Alone—alone, in eve's dream-dusk!
In the thicket whose tender young boughs sighed sad.
   With no wood-rose, whose heavy musk
Would have drear'ly tranced me in dreams we had.

When thine eyes, abashed, would turn from mine—
When thy voice was so faint—thy grace divine!

Through wild-entangled twigs I strolled—
In the wail of the muttering, sad-voiced brook—
　A mystic murmur o'er the wold—
And a ghastly sound, heard from ghostly crook.
And the dying glow-sky—the various trees—
Were sweet-cradled, in the brook, by the lower breeze!

　Then back to bourne of that gloom-brake—
On a field, I gazed at the calm gold moon!
　While softly-wailing winds did wake
Those sweet smiles of thine, that near winter-noon,
When it pleased thee to ask of former days—
When thy voice seemed the strains of love-lulled lays!

O wind! that breathed a lusty breath—
All thy flow from South—where she fares at home.
　O had you borne what her heart saith
When alone she is—and no one to come
To be soothing her smart, to redden her cheek—
None to court her—with her of Love to speak!

　Two violets I held in my hand—
While the tinkling bells were so drear'ly swelling—
　The bird was perched on apple-wand—
While on high the moon glowed, the stars were knelling

All their gold bells ! and days with no violet
Me consumed—and my heart was one regret !

    Two purple violets I found
By the logs where leaves lie so brown and sear,
    Upon the Spring-blessed leaf-strown ground—
Where the brooklet washed the eve's trailing gear—
And it splashed it away ! I heard in its spray
Her bright laughter that made me love that day !

    Fair violets, sweet memories !
Oh ! pervade the blossoms, the breeze-shaken wolds!
    And when I walk upon the leas,
O'er the hills, down slopes, o'er the paths, through folds
Live before my own love-gaze—fume the scene!
Color hills purplier—the meadows thrice as green !
    WILLIAM'S FARM, ITHACA, N. Y.

"IN THE DUSK THIS LAY WAS BORN."

TENDER Anne! at my beloved hour 'twas, I
    strolled
  Along the hedgèd gray hill-side;
Then up a winding road, 'long a gloomy wold
  Tenanted by shocking shapes at eventide!
(With thy spirit I walked;
To thine invisable ears I talked!)
At my beloved hour! when the pines are gilded,
    Anne.
When glows the calm eve-air; and the moon is
    flushèd, Anne.

O Charming Anne! through dells the drear path
    dropt;
  Then beckoned the highway dreamily.
Passed copse, to cottage came, then sudden stopt:
  To list to clear purls in an orchard-tree.
(With thy thoughts I communed;
With thy tender smile the purls were more sweetly
    tuned!)
More more the road-side gloomed, and the branches
    held light fays.
Sweet-purpled the mountain far; the white lilacs
    fumed their lays!

"In the Dusk This Lay Was Born." 61

Lovely Anne! I clomb a hillock to its crest;
   Inhaled the air o'er all the hills,
Some netted trees were darkning the red west—
   And sweetly twittered birds, in peeps and trills.
(Oh! once I heard thy girly smile;
Thy grace, so tender, joyed me all the while!)
Far in the valley haze, the dim town sparkled all her gems.
As though good angels watched; in their curls pure diadems.

Oh! passionate Anne! Above the distant height
   A moon rose: solid sardonyx!
She cut the dark purple mist, that hid her light—
   As though the moon and mist would wildly mix!
(Thy heart was near to mine
For I felt a heart-throb, while no moon did shine!)
I saw the massive moon; when she glowed alone— a queen!
She veiled her face—then gleamed—till her cheeks were a sallow sheen!

Only Anne! How calm, ineffably serene
   The air, the west, the east, the wolds!
How few delight in: when the mystic scene
   Itself in shrouds of star-spelled night enfolds!
(How hankered I after thy pure hand;
To clasp mine warmly, while the songs were all so bland!)

I trod the homeward way! in the dusk this lay was
    born!
Belovèd strolls may wind where the scene is weird
    and lorn!
WILLIAMS'S FARM, ITHACA, N. Y.

"WITH ALL MY HEART I WISHED THAT
YOU WERE THERE."

WITH all my heart I wished that you were
        there—
    By the sweet gurgling meadow-brook;
With chasing merls—and blackbirds in the air;
    A splashing mere around the crook—
And meadow-larks ahopping on the bray,
    Or rustling in their shady nook.
Green banks of tasselled willows hid the view away;
And drumming quail afar, that drummed for
        dying May!

All afternoon it snowed on me, my dear—
    While all the stones were warm and bright.
The flakes were blown way to the sounding wear
    All while the sun poured down his light!

IN THE DUSK THIS LAY WAS BORN . . . .
Page 62.

"I Wished That You Were There." 63

It snowed—but no white sheet lay on the ground.
　The flakes that fell were lost to sight,
When the bland breeze blew them away! O Anne! astound,
　The tasselled willows sowed their seeds without a sound!

How sad am I, that you, sweet, could not share
　With me that tender afternoon!
It was the time, when all the willows wear
　A delicate green; an early moon
Wafts on their wooly flowers her gilded song.
　When hazels bud; the wild-vine's rune
Flows down their twigs; when peaceful clouds the pale blue throng.
When all is joyous; all is witched by May's dear song!

And Anne, thrice hummed that dear sweet throat, and whirred
　Its filmy wings—and poised in air!
It was the golden-necklaced humming-bird
　That thrummed, and twanged—and seemed so fair!
Its long beak drank the nectar from lone flowers,
　That hung like scarlet bells down there!
How flightily it drank! all poising on short hours—
Then swiftly thrummed away—to seek full fairer bowers!

O Anne! were you there, when I culled their bloom,
  My wordings would have woven slim
To tender fancies—flown from Flora's loom!
  Five scarlet horns, with golden brim,
Hath he to sip his wine from—silk-decked horns,
  With mead-brimmed sacks, and red bands trim!
And while he quaffs, a tuft of lemon plumes adorns
His sky—and from some pillage-bee his small ear
    warns!

The shadows laid their long forms on the sand—
  And blazing was the burning West!
And lone I trod the bray—with no soft hand
  To touch my longing thoughts to rest!
I watched the waters come—then babble—then fall
  Adown a log—to a snake's nest,
Then flow in wider bed;—I saw a serpent small
Relish the spray—then sudden flash—and that was
    all!

The snuffling waters rushed—a sough made moan.
  A fish leapt from his brook-bred weed;
Soused in the shallow stream—and then swam on.
  A sheld snake left a glittering brede
Behind, as it wound through the drowsy shade.
  The rocking breeze bent the tall reed,
And clarified the purls from distant bowery glade—
And, Anne! a purer spirit from high on me was
    laid!

Oh! how the evening would have gladder sung,
  If, with thy warble, my path led
Me past the lazy barns, where pigeons young
  Were fluttering; where swallows fled
From eaves—and winged the balmy breath of day!
  Past blossomed trees, all white, or red.
Past chanticleers, that wistful guard their hens—
    past spray
Of lilac white, past kine, and farmyard fray!
WILLIAMS'S FARM, ITHACA, N. Y.

"SHE WAS A NINETEENTH-CENTURY LAMIA."

WAS she a Lamia, dight in maiden-raiments,
  When she first had startled my love-gone
    eye!
Had she the serpent-born's sweet wiles and magic,
  Her own luring glance and her warm moist eye!
And when she saw me in her wild web strangled
  She had calmed her passion, and trancèd me
To love her as a saint would love a woman:
  Soul and heart true tendered with purity!

Was she a Lamia, with a witching body,
  When she first had sparkled the morning's hour!

With all her serpent spell to sweet entice me
   To entangle me well in her tender power!
When I held my heart high above her tresses
   When she knew that I was in love and wild—
Then I was forced by flames that burst my heart-
      wound
   To be hers, though she only played and smiled!

Was she a Lamia, tender as a maiden,
   With heart-speaking eyes, and a smile of truth!
With holiness of soul shown on her forehead—
   From all falsehood far and so rich in ruth!
And when I caught each silvery purl and golden,
   From two roses red, moulded to her mouth—
She saw she won me—then she hated, scoffed me—
   And my heart was burnt by a fire of south!

Was she a Lamia—in her heart a serpent—
   To delude—allure me to her amorous side!
When she had showed sweet signs of love-affec-
      tions—
   When she sent a love-glance, and then had tried
To seek for my own eye—had heard my whis-
      pers—
   Then when laughing long in her dimpled cheek
That I was in her spell—she scorned me, and
      proudly
   Did avert her gaze—would not laugh or speak!

A SKETCH FOR HANNAH . . . .

Page 67.

A Lamia?—Yea, a nineteenth-century Lamia—
With a pride, a flirt, and a spell in her face.
But spite of all her serpent-stealing temper—
She will e'er remain my own lovable grace!
For all my heart is aglow—a lasting ember!
   And it stings! though she has not wished me stay.
Oh, truth! if sun-rays shine through stormy even,
So her love will gleam on a future day!
LONG ISLAND, N. Y.

A SKETCH FOR HANNAH.

THIS morn I found a simple brooklet-scene,
   Aft' wandering long, and luring hundred sheep
About me—how they bleated, huddled, stared
At seeing such bold trespasser on their field!
And Hannah sweet! the distant trees are blue—
There peep some chimneys through the tall osage,
Whose slender stems are graceful; 'bout the brook
Are white and silver willows, and osiers golden,
Still blooming their wool-catkins: boon of Spring!
And, ere the warm green waters find a crook,
A weathered fence outruns the rich-blue shade

Of silvered, shivering shrubs—then bends its
    boards;
And, swooning in the herbs and golden flowers,
Just breaks a bonny wavelet near the pebbles;
From there the breded waters are swift hidden
By one virescent sweep of meadow-land!
And, dear one, over all this Spring-kissed scene
A blessing sentinel—a leafless tree,
Drooped so almost to touch the far horizon,
Does breathe to those young tender shrubs and
    stems
A language, eloquent of by-gone days—
A tongue that tells that, though the osiers golden,
The silvery willows, and the grace-osage
May green from year to year—the blossomed past
That hath no pulsings more, sprouts never leaves,
Nor buds its blossoms—but the ages gone
May stand on the gray track of memory
And speak of deeds that were, and hopes that
    bloomed,
As the black bark and weathered blea unfold
The days when that tree's slender stems were green!

And lovely Hannah! one dim day may give
Me you! and then this sketch, that I will keep
With all its colors soft, its sparkling lights,
May joy your eyes—may woo from your fond lips
A pure love kiss, that speaks how true and deep
You love your faithful lover, loving you!

The sweet *bree-reeing* blackbird, perched on twigs
Of tender osiers, that shade the long marsh-grass;--
The clear purl, flowing from the blue-bird, swinging
On vines that dream on rustic hedge;—the cheep
Of catbirds, chasing through tangled willow-withes;—
The distant, tremulous throatings of sweet birds;—
All, all those simple strains evoked this dream
That whispered: Hannah will be yours! And Anne!
Above soul's golden brim, my bliss spilled over!
   WILLIAMS'S FARM, ITHACA, N. Y.

THE WORKINGS OF THE SOUL.

OH! wonderful, unutterably sweet—
   The workings of the loving soul—
      A thousand times my Hannah I may meet:
   In the fragrant woodlands of my soul!

Oh! charmful, all-unutterably fond—
   The kindness of the loving soul:
My Hannah walks with me to skies beyond—
   Then steps through green groves of my soul!

Oh! wonderful, unutterably sweet—
  The workings of the loving soul—
A thousand times my Hannah I may meet:
  In the redolent rose-fields of my soul!
LONG ISLAND, N. Y.

DARKNESS GROWS LUMINOUS WHEN THINKING OF THEE.

AS I paced the pavement of the dusk-draped city,
  . The west it was flushed with a pink and pur-
    ple and red—
For the stars began shining, and the sun he was
    dead.
I thought of my love—and my heart it fought with
    a yearning:
Like fire in a lovely bush it was burning!
  I thought of my love; my heart beat; my cheeks
    they tingled;
My soul it was lustrous, and haloed by wondrous
    light!
My feet leapt, as if driven by sudden affright;
  For the sky that was red—it was gone! the dusk
    had mingled
With the west, and town and spires were leering at
    night!

* * * * * *

Then methought there streamed o'er me a singular flood,
That spent an odor, to awe me, and curdle my blood!
Away, ye!—Grim phantoms spilt opiate-thrilled phials
  O'er roofs and streets, o'er spires, o'er people and me.
Then they thronged about steeples, and laughed, all turning the dials,
And played with the time, and pushed the church-towers;
Then rained such sulphurous-scented showers,
That clave to my brow—and my eyes they grew wide!—
  They sought for the seraph-shape of saint— Sanctity!

* * * * * *

But the vision it vanished of sudden—I thought of my love—
And the great, good God that was laboring above!
  Oh! the mysterious influence of paly-palled time!
When the essence of nature laves chillingly your cheek,
  Then the soul surrenders to life that is only sublime—
Then each speck of dark, and of light an awe-tongue speak,

Then the lips they do kiss the drear of the hour
  —till a tune,
Like from flutes in a dusky grove, is born—and it
  haunts the step!
  When the liquid lispings from the bare tree-
    branches rune
And linger about your locks, whisper wonders in
  your ear—
Then your eyes they grow large as those of a seer:
  When he's in fumes of witching oils, and herbs,
    and nep!
There, in your weird-warbled strain you may hear
  The wails of departed—they who have battled on
    bloody mounds;
  The sighs of dejected, who've loved, and lived,
    and have nursed their wounds;
Then the warble grows passionate—like the sway of
    pine-trees so drear
  Draws passion athrough the brown needles when
    Autumn's wild moan sounds!
In the warm chill of the dusk to wander away—
  Alone—with but a thought of your love.
You see the phantoms peopling the skies so gray—
  But you know there's a wondrous light above!
Oh! Love! what a solace to the dusk-wandering
    dreamer's fear-sight:
*Those thousand grim spectres seem ten thousand angels
    in white!*

Oh! Love, the truest test of God,
Love, walking with a myrtle-rod!
My love! however dark the evening-sod—
  'Twill flame to green if you are in my thought!
LONG ISLAND, N. Y.

"IF THE FLOWERS KNEW IT."

OH! if the flowers of the fields—
  If they knew it, if they knew it!
They would fold their petals to their morning-
  buds—
And the fields they would feel many minion-floods.
Oh! if the wild-wood flowers—
If they knew it, if they knew it!
The orchid would stand without a queenly crown.
The lone anemones would hang their petals down!
And the violets would peep no more;
Nor the bluets by the balmy shore.
And the star-flowers would fade—
The smocks, the fox-bells, in the sunny glade!
Oh! all would droop their heads, and all would die,
If they knew how alone with my misery am I!
Oh! if the flowers of the gardens,
If they knew it, if they knew it!

Oh! the pink would pale; the rose would be red not—
The asters cloud their heaven; the dahlia would wed not!
The heliotrope be scentless—the fuxia would faint,—
And all the gorgeous blooms would be heavy with plaint.
If they knew it, the gardens would fume from tears—
And each flower would mourn for many years!
   Long Island, N. Y.

SONG TO MINE ANGELS.

O ANGELS! fly to her—
  And tell that her wooer,
    Through day, and dreary night
Hath borne his doleful plight!
Oh! strew white lilies over her—
With scented vairs do cover her!
Let roses red rain through
Her chamber so odorous;
Let not a sharp pain through,
Nor troubles, so onerous.
Be playing your fiddles

Song to Mine Angels.

As symphonies of glory—
And tell her those riddles,
That sheen our life's story!
Let no animosity
Be stirring her tender heart—
Let couth generosity
See that no Love-sender part!
For she is a fairy!
She's all so unwary
That red o'er her dimples floods!
For she is a flower,
That opened an hour
Before the plant's other buds!
O angels, she's esteemed.
Her carriage is queenly—
She walks, as Hannah deemed:
Fearless and serenely!
O angels she is maidenly—
And hoppeth as Nycheia—
With her April-like eyes;
And though her form all laden be
With beauties like Maia—
She's mine for the skies!
Pray! therefore fly to her
And whisper: her wooer
Is singing in silent longing!
And whisper: she's sweet—
For me more than meet—
While memories my heart are thronging!
O angels, soft cover her—

Strew lilies all over her;
Chaste thoughts through her hair-locks
Be guiding them so silently!
Through the tangles of her fair-locks
Flow purest streams of Love's sweet glee!
Oh! sing to her symphonies!
Oh! chant to her prophesies!
Oh! keep her, as the rose in forests!
Oh! see that her dear loving so rests
That all its languors are for me!
O angels! be singing;
O angels! be bringing
My love to her heart!
O angels! be sending—
O angels! be bending
Your bow for the arrow—
Your shaft that is narrow—
To pierce her a smart!
Oh! know her worthy of Heaven!
And tell her *she* hath been given
To him who loves Eternity!

LONG ISLAND, N. Y.

LOVE'S PUREST JOY.

IT is balm, that floweth down Hymettus-mount—
It is perfume, sweet-exhaled by Aegle's fount!
It is fragrance, shed from Flora's flower-shades—
It is sweetness, from fair Ceres' golden glades!
It is air that blows coy Zephyrus through Olympos-
    pines!
It is like the rush, and flush, they heard, and saw
    by Bachus' wines!
It is mystical as were the songs in wise Dodona's
    grove.
It is richer than the Paphian sound, where Venus
    dreamed of love.

It is fresher than the fabled Hippocrene—
It is goldier-spun, than gold-leaves, that were
    seen,
  When firy Helios wandered through his cherished
    tree!
It is fancyful as tales that lost Ulysses told
  To Nausicaa, of princesses sweetest she!
It is rapturous as garland-dances of the Oread.
Dithyrambic more than Satyr-revels in the wold
    Where Silenus, maudlin, lay asleep in evening-
        shade!

More than all those sweets of Greece, of goddesses,
    of gods—
Is that purest joy I feel, *when Annie's self—*
She my beaming, only pretty dearest maiden-elf—
Cometh dancing, blushing over thought's sweet-bloom-
    ing sods.
LONG ISLAND, N. Y.

O DOVE!

O DOVE! my heart is thy nest—
    My soul is thy sky—
Wherein thou mayest find rest;
Wherethrough thou mayst fly!

O dove! make in me thy home—
    Around me thy heaven!
Wherein to blossom thy doom—
    So e'er be love-driven!

O dove! about me be e'er!
    My heart and my soul
Are nest and sky, both so fair,
    For thee—to life's goal!

LONG ISLAND, N. Y.

IN MEASURES—GRACEFUL AS THE THREE!

SUDDEN MUSIC CAME ASTREAMING.

O HANNAH! how the cadence falls, so gladly!
   In measures—graceful as the three!
Oh! now it dances—sweetly-toned—so madly—
   She gleamed—sweet mirth—Euphrosyne!

O Hannah! how melodiously flows the song!
   Oh! tuned to jollity and laughter.
Oh! tripped not fair Thalia's playful throng—
   With rosy-cheeked sweet virgins after!

Hannah! thy dapper feet may not enjoy
   Such Corymbanthian dancing-time!
Oh! come in spirit! garbed as Love's decoy,
   That moved in groves of Delos' clime!

O Hannah! how the cadence fell, so gladly—
   In measures—graceful as the three.
Oh! how it danced—so sweetly-toned—so madly—
   She gleamed—sweet mirth—Euphrosyne!
INTERVALE, WHITE MTS., N. H.

LOVE'S MOOD.

THE lover, as an everblushing rose,
   That by a fairy-glade's lone arbor grows,
  Is silent when his flower hath not bloomed,
As when the breeze the glade hath not perfumed.
He still hath blushings on his doubting cheeks,
As rose still smiles her pinkish-huèd streaks.
For ever all before his gaze he gathers all her
    charms—
Thus lulling to calm sleep his anxioux love-alarms!

Oh! she bloomed not for many, fretful days!
Her fresh rose-dimples, like those of morning-fays,
Spelled me in no sweet trance—like Houri-spells.
Like Houri-lips, her own no syllables
Uttered to me; her eyes, so laughing, bright—
Laughed not in mine to find a kindred loving light.
My love, the glowing-cheeked, who witched me to
    her side,
Would she be willing wreathe herself mine Angel-
    bride!

Oh! would that o'er the span o' my loving soul
A vision I could see: o' a flowery knoll
With violets, forget-me-nots o'ergrown—
And tall grass, by a soothing South-wind blown

Love's Mood.

To wavy bendings ! on the summit, pines,
That dusk the sky that flames in orange lines !
And in among the flowers and grass would stately smile—
Oh ! she—whose loadstar-eyes my musing thought beguile !

What plaint the lover's longing for her breeds!
On what dim hope the lover's waiting feeds!
'Tis sweet the love he bears to her fair bower,
And even if she no love to him doth dower—
The fragrance that his vision's nosegay wafts
Is same as one of Cupid's myrtle-shafts!
'Tis rapture when, in dreams, he sees her grace divine—
And feels her influence by his wizard-side recline!
LONG ISLAND, N. Y., 1885.

SPRING'S VOICELESS RAIN.

THE far, blue hills, pale as the palest sky,
   When high the frore-smoke pales the autumn's
    dome!
Are in the Season's transformation's womb:
A warmer shroud of gray!—Rare murmurs try
To startle Silence: from the bare boughs hie
   The robin and oriole: one sings of home—
   One feigns the ecstasy of Spring; by tomb
Of Winter the lizard sings as Joy were by!

A voiceless rain! whose drops but eagle's eyne
   May scarce discern—so fine, so delicate—
Like spray of perfume where the suckles twine!
   A toneless mizzle—invisible—like fate!
So Annie! stream upon the mourning heart
Soft tears unseen, unheard—never to part!
   NEW JERSEY.

A LOVER'S REQUEST.

AGAIN those clear, cool mornings bring the tones
   Of other worlds, where love is contemplation—
   Again the sun—by arctic concentration,
Is drawn: to take from winter's throat those groans,
That shrieked, or chafed! to fill the airy lones
   With carols, breezes: love's sweet delectation!
   To kiss, with warmer lip, the spirit's nation!
And flow the streams with jubilant undertones!

Oh! Birth of Life! that slept these thirty weeks!
   And will that blander air revive her love
Of former days, when she had bloomed her cheeks!
   When she, in bashful way, to win me strove!
Oh! fling thy fragrance, balmy air of Spring!
To her love-heart—and thrill her soul, to sing!

LONELINESS.

AY, little villous mouse,
    Hast left thy little house,
    To keep me company!
Ay, shy, small hider thou!
Hast come beguiling me
With such quaint drolery:
Of runnings—gazings——wow!—
And why so swiftly gone—
All leaving me alone!
Hast thou then known that I
Was pining here so longingly!
To peep into the room—
And gaze into my face of gloom!
But why not stay—and play with me,
For I dream here so mournfully!
Ay, little, villous mouse—
Why back into thy little house!
Thy droleries would fill the quiet room—
And I could better bear my fated doom!
But come again, dear mouse! so droll and
    small—
  I shall not kill thee—surely—not at all!

LONG ISLAND, N. Y.

"SHE IS FAIREST."

OH! she is fairest
    In all the land!
  Oh! she is dearest,
    With face so bland—
With cheeks as campion blown in showers;
    With blissful eyes—
    That love the azure skies!
    And sweet-voiced lips
    Whereon a love-bee sips,
Beguiling long and dreary hours!
  Oh! she is sweetest
    To woo her hand!
  Oh! she is meetest
    All to command!

LONG ISLAND, N. Y.

VAIN WISHES.

I WISH I were a butterfly
   To flutter about her winsome head—
  Upon her cherry-lips to lie
   And suck and suck, till I were dead!
Oh! butterfly! be wary where thou liest, where thou diest!
But flutter aye about her: she the wisest and the shyest!

I wish I were the evening-breeze—
   That playeth in her fairy-hair!
Would whisper her a dream-surcease,
   And build therein my life-long lair.
Oh! evening-breeze! take me on thine invisible breath, that whispereth;
And let me stay there in her blowing curls, till death, till death!

I wish I were the perfume pure
   Within the rose that warms her bosom!
Fling ope' the gold-walls, that immure,
   Within her soul, love's bashful blossom!
Oh! perfume pure! like opiate scents bask me in thy scent, so innocent!
Take me within her soul, that she'll be love-lorn bent—that she'll consent!

I wish I were the wee wee bee—
That drones, through June, to the wild wood-
    rose !—
Beneath her lily-buds would be—
Sting—till her heart as an ember glows !
Oh ! wee, wee bee ! uplift thy wing, and let me
    guide thee, to mine own fair !
And I shall tell thee sting and sting, till her heart
    wear my deep love's vair !

A LIGHTNING-MOMENT OF RAPTURE.

OH! to steal into the heart
    Of Annie, she in love !
  Lie there—never to depart—
    And ever lovelier prove:
What happiness ! what joy, bliss, rapture—oh !
    what glow !
More splendor-weal than June-bird, winging to and
    fro,
    Hath in the orange-bosks, where glides,
      Low under, golden water !
  And by the blooms—on all the side
      Sweet maidens, with their laughter,

Thrill all the languid sounds, that play in tune—
Thrill all the pulses of warm-hearted June!
  Oh! to linger lovingly
    Down where her heart-throbs croon—
  Oh! to die there glad and free!
  Would be my highest boon!
LONG ISLAND, N. Y.

THE RARE INFLUENCE OF MUSIC.

THE perfect pianist plays the prelude—
  The all-attentive audience thrills—
The glowing house is gairish modelled—
  Attention all the audience fills!

'Tis some concerto that he's playing—
  With skill, and art, and feeling mixed.
Some weird wild melodies its passion—
  Full-deep achordes are strong infixed!

'Tis, as the prayers of old, the warriors
  Loud chanted, ere the fires flamed—
Then dies, and melts within the breathings
  Of maidens, for their valor famed!

It softens, as the far-off singing
  Of virgins, by the Vishnu-sea!
Then swelleth, as when Baal came faring
  O'er lands to the Phoenecian lea!

It flows, as passionate desire—
  As Pan, fleet-footing Syrinx fair—
It purleth low, as prating Oreads
  While braiding their long golden hair!

There hung upon those chordes so hollow—
  A curse, as lone Kehama bore!
Then angels hovered—hymning—singing
  A benediction evermore!

It was a concert, quaint and colored!
  The pianist played in perfect way—
The audience answered all the passion
  He poured into the fancy-lay!

I mused in Music's melodious mansion—
  I lost my memory in the strain—
And with the dreamy, witching flowing
  Forgot my longing's wretched pain!

On pillows plumed with Angel-feathers,
  I leaned my heavy head, to stare
With languid eyes into Elysium,
  And gaze on faces fair and rare. . . .

*   *   *   *   *

What see my dream-eyes in the gold-box—
　　How wide their lids are burst apart !
Oh ! there she dreams; oh ! there my loved-one
　　Sweet converse holds with her pure heart !

Our eyes they meet ! . . . she flames to burning—
　　She heaves—and is a flowery sea
Of blossoming beauties in exultation
　　Whose bloomed emotion swells for me !

She leaps the velvet—I leap the audience !
　　She hovers the wild harmonies o'er—
Within mine arms I clasp her beauty—
　　In time to be her savior !

As Ella, with her swans, ascending
　　The skies, to greet the angel host—
So rise our shapes, in love-embracement,
　　Till from the melodies are lost !

As pale Francesca met her lover
　　Above the quiet midnight-towers—
And fast to heart and loving bosom
　　They rose to Heaven's joying bowers—

So twined, in slow-dissoloing windings
　　Our beating hearts and pressèd lips—
Toward that far realm of lover's longing
　　Where God His loving children keeps !

　　　*　　*　　*　　*　　*

The Rare Influence of Music.

The pianist plays with perfect purlings—
 The all-attentive audience thrills—
The glowing house is glittering fashioned—
 Attention all the audience fills !

'Tis a concerto quaint and colored—
 The last songs fade, and treble soft.
Applause is laughing through the audience—
 And I have fallen from aloft!

'Twas a prelude, wild and languid—
 Dear lays—a deep pathetic tune.
As smote the thunder the huge cloud-zone;
 As sweetly smiled the tears of June!

And have I clasped my love in visions!
 Upbore the angels two love-clays!
Oh! music dreams—and dreamers listen—
 And love is tuneful dream always!

The pianist played—the audience listened—
 I dreamed—she leapt adown to me—
In love-strong arms I bore her beauty
 To Heaven! . . . And was all vanity!
NEW YORK, N. Y.

MEMORIES, SWEET, YET SORE!

OH! lull me to sleep,
    You baby-wavelets of the deep!
      That break upon the gently-shelving sand;
  In murmurous melodies then die:
  As even the beadings of a memory:
Far, far in fairer scenes—in a fairer land!

    Oh! lull me to sleep,
    You creeping wavelets of the deep!
Across the straits the misty mountains loom;
  While o'er the sea the vessels fly:—
  Alas, portending one high memory;
Alas, my wandering, all unresting doom!

    Oh! lull me to sleep
    You wavelets of the blue, calm deep!
Mewould my thought could mingle with your play
  Be borne away, upon your seaward-song!
  As e'en the memories that e'er will throng
My soul, sweet given to her, whom I love alway!

    Oh! lull me to sleep,
    You baby-wavelets of the deep!

ACROSS THE STRAITS THE MISTY MOUNTAINS LOOM . . . . .

That break upon the gently-shelving sand;
In slow surge faint—in murmurs, die,
Oh! so mewould *one* burning memory—
Far far in a virgin home—in a paradise-land!
MESSINA, SICILY, ITALY.

LOVE'S HISTORY REPEATS ITSELF.

O LOVE hast read of Valentine
And Sylvia, his love divine!
They loved, as we some years ago.
And he was banished from his love,
Because he wilfully would go
And see his Sylvia unobserved:
At night—with ladder, through the grove,
And scale the wall; yet he had failed—
Was exiled to the Mantuan woods!
So was our love; our actions swerved;
O'er all the world I roamed—and sailed:
An exile, in love's solitudes!
What Proteus is now courting thee ?!
Or dost, like Sylvia, think of me!
Methought Shakespeare's own thought had dreamed
His play—alas! it is too true:

The love we bore, when loving seemed
As living as the morning's hue!
And all the action in his play
Seems like thy love—and my dismay!
  NEW YORK, N. Y.

LOVE IS THE CREATOR.

ALL lay in chaos, sluggish—undefined—
  God let His love be born—all worlds were made!
So was the soul of man inactive—sloth—resigned—
  Till Love built our civilization's upward grade!
  NEW YORK, N. Y.

END OF LOVE-BLOSSOMS.

SONGS OF SPRING.

SPRING IS HERE.

WRITTEN IN MY BOYHOOD.

OH! now is the time when all the trees are ablooming
  With smiles of a blending glow! The shrubs are asprouting
And, burdened with leaves, they glisten in glow of the sunshine
Yes, now the low apple-tree goggles with thousand of eyelets
That blend the surrounding branches; shedding a glowing
Wide atmosphere round and round! And, now and then smiling,
Their cheek in a guaze of pinkish hue, they seem envious
Of cherry-tree, wild and standing near to their fireside.
The apple-trees, the pear-trees, plum—and all of their family,
Fill orchards with fragrance, paint them daringly gorgeous,
Bring sweet and strange savor to airs that confront them.

The orchards are full of tinges that May, with artistic
Soft hand hath, in wondrous time, arrayed with her pigments:
Her pigments of verdure, blending white, and of yellow,
A yellow that kisses more green than yolk of an egglet!
Not sole are the orchards doomed to bear all the glory
Of May-time! In every nook, and rent, of the country
Bright May doth endow the growths with splendor proportionate.
'Neath stones of a tinge that tells of long and wild ages
Lone whiteling Clematis droops her head with oblations
To May! under leaves all withered, sere, from last Autumn,
Arbutus doth twine her limbs with wondrous dexterity;
And thrusts out her head, coquettishly, blooming with vagaries!
The charm of the wood's wild lones, the cherry of Spring-tide,
Now too doth beredden its savory head, which, engirdled
By three of the leaflets, glazy, shining, green and soft brown-red,

Spring is Here.

Invites the lone wanderer to rest, and taste its clean flavor !
And, peeping from craggy hills, the yellow lone lily
Doth bend her bespotted neck in awe of Queen Mayling !
Extending her tender arms above her head's bowings
And filling the dreamer with cravings, bent to be-rob her.
Close by, in a hollow, families, nestled in sweet dalliance,
Love's violets besprinkle the green, with brown intermingled—
Where rocks are abounding, stars of white shine above them—
On lank and lone stems they rest—and joy the weird wanderer !
And even the moss takes vivid color ! clothes the old log-barks
With velvet; and draws upon them red or gray excrescences.
Now back to fair fields and highways, trimmed for the season:
Our eyes do meet all the wonders that moon of the leaves lends !
There grows, in the shade of grasses, the tooth of the gold-lion—
'Neath yonder low mound the saxifrage is awooing
Soft breezes, that flit around with softening blushes!
The cow-slips revive their former beauty and meekness.

All growths that the fields hail in times of the Child-
    ling,
Abundantly pay their homage to her with kindness;
And 'mong those created children at play in their
    innocence
Soft larvae of beetles, of butterflies, and gold hum-
    ble-bees,
Perch now on some stem of grass, and then are
    afalling
Adown to the softened turf, and there enjoy a fat
    feasting !
    ITHACA, N. Y. 1883.

MAY-DITTY.

FLY, fly, fly—
    Happy May! abloom !
Fly, fly, fly !
Thy zephyrs blow !
Soft samiels grow—
With all aglow
Will flee thy foe !
Fly, fly, fly,
Merry May ! abloom!
Fly, fly, fly !

May-Ditty.

Waft, waft, waft,
Scented May ! thy tang !
Waft, waft, waft !
Through azure sky
Fair birdies fly !
Send forth thy spy—
Bid frost: " good-bye ! "
Waft, waft, waft—
Musky May ! thy tang !
Waft, waft, waft !

Linger, linger, linger,
Mazy May ! long, long !
Linger, linger, linger—
Near garden's gate—
'Neath hoary fate—
Adorn thy state—
Remain elate !
Linger, linger, linger,
Verdant May ! long, long !
Linger, linger, linger !

Fly, fly, fly,
Virgin May ! aslow !
Fly, fly, fly
With measured wing—
Let nature ring !
Let mortals sing
To Heaven's King !

Fly, fly, fly,
Saintly May! aslow!
Fly, fly, fly!
ITHACA, N. Y. 1883

TO MINE OCARINO.

AN ITALIAN WIND-INSTRUMENT.

HAST lain so friendlessly
   Without the memory
 Of one, who loved thee once,
As, many years gone, Ponce
De Leon loved his vessel fine,
That bore him oft through storm and shine
To wolds luxuriantly grown
Where Mexico's salubrious winds are blown!
And have I quite forgotten now
That once you were the Prow
To Pleasure's Barge, my childhood cherished,
When yet my glow-hope had not perished;
That you were my sole joy
When all had called me boy
Of dreamy wildness—shunning study,
But blooming in wild nature, ruddy
And nature-like ! Oh! have the days
Grown so that they prompt no fair lays:

WHERE SALMACIS YET DWELLED ALONE.

Page 103.

To Mine Ocarino.

What once my child-like bliss was;
What once my maiden's kiss was.
Then would I pipe sweet ditties:
For, far from noise and cities,
Where Salmacis yet dwelled alone
And had not heard the moan
Of Aphroditus' love—to chain
Her heart to throes, and lover's pain.
And now, in philosophic days,
Has death clutched all thy beauty-lays;
Of sheep-folk; and of purses
Peach-glowed; and tangled thyrses
That some boozed swain upbore
To signal: "More, oh! more!"
Have meditations, deeper
Than man's immortal Reaper,
Effaced the memories
Of thy soft melodies:
Sweet-mating with the matin-songs,
The lark in morn's mid-heaven throngs,
To herald: higher, higher
Is a world of sweeter fire:
A song without an end—
A life with love-lipped friend!
Oh! have these longing hours
Of love outtuned the showers
Of cheery tibial cadences—
Piped all to quicken the maid-dances
'Neath glowing oaks, when Hesper
Has prayed, and sung her vesper.

These days of wild despair,
Have they neglected thy sweet air:
Assembling once the wings
Near forest-brooks, to listen to things
But superstitious ears would hear
Upon a lea, ghost-wild and drear.

Mine Ocarino, friend of mine!
When, from the rigid line
Of students, I had sped
To mossy brooks—where Limniads tread
O'er glassy pool; and Fauns
Upspring, like startled fawns,
To catch their Satyr-brothers;
Where lonely Echo smothers
Within some long-cut gash,
(Where lily-goblins dash,)
For one who died for her—
Where all is one sweet stir
Of myth, and fancy fair—
'Twas there, my friend! 'Twas there
I blew within thee melody:
The forest's lonely ecstasy.
I knew that loneliness
Was not like world's distress:
But sylvan shades are sweeter,
And brooks and bosks are meeter—
Than all the store of tomes,
Within the learnéd homes

Of wallèd knowledge!—go
To realms of *sapient glow:*
Where nature broods in thought!
Without her, lore is naught!

*   *   *   *   *

I recollect the morns
When, passed the woodland-thorns,
I wandered, breaking twigs,
And chasing whirligigs,
To where the brook-lime shines
Its flowers in azure lines.
And sanicles upbear
Their heads: Quick cure is here!
Where spiders lonely spin;
And where the winnows win
A wavelet—to breathe the air—
To feel the sun, and see sweet nature there!
And where the rabbit oft
Doth prick his ears, so soft.
Where, singing, dips a beak—
Resprinkles the crispèd creek!
Where flit the orange orioles,
And perch on reeds, like festive poles
With dimly-burning flambeaux peaked!
The red-black marsh-bird, sweet bree-reeing
In joy—and swaying—swiftly fleeing;—
Thence I clomb some lonely holt
With sear leaves, whom flowers streaked—

There sported the horse and colt—
And, where no sun did shine,
Drowsily the lilling kine
Closed eyes—and, where the pine
And birch, and alder a concert tune,
Skipped ever Nymph-like June!
Then I adown a glacis leapt—
Where wild-flowers sweet trysting places kept,
Where all the insects chirred—
Where fairy-lays linger'd
Such sweetest brooklet gleamed,
Till in its song I dreamed!
Then all upon some rock,
With sable-green, and redlined frock,
I sat—and there I piped,
And piped, and piped, and piped—
Till birdlings quite outsung
The ditties I had swung.
Then nature, Spring-born, glowed;
And each sweet piping showed
A long-drawn vista—painted
With landscape, unacquainted
To those who shape their day
With stones, and ore, and clay!
There sat I, all alone—
With rushings, and a tone
Or wild delight:
The brooklet's bickering flight!
Oh! there thou wast my friend,

To Mine Ocarino.

My youthful, rapturous friend!
Who made me young, and made
Sweet rapture run through all the glade!
Oh! Ocarino, simple instrument,
Then to a grove of oaks I went—
That spread its branches wide
To one gloom-steep—the pride
Of vale, and one loud waterfall.
There called I all the birds, did thrall
The breezes to my bonny tune;
In blissful honey-June!
And there the goat-herds browsed—
And oft a gudgeon sowzed:
Delusion for the falcon's eye,
Who winged the bright blue sky!
And there the miller's daughter strayed—
And beckoned, from the vale's cool shade;
And there the bees came humming by—
Or cleaved to flower that winks its eye!
And songs we heard, as from cuckoos come,
By Bradmere, a poet's fondest home!
Oh! there I blew within thy mould—
I piped like they of old,
When Galatea strung a wreath
For couth Pygmalion—
When panting bosom, hurried breath,
Announced a love-talk—all alone!
When shepherds dreamed—and maids
Knew nought of shameful raids.

When fair Estelle wept bitter tears
For one, to battle gone for years—
When she was fain to die—
But sudden, her wet eye
Beheld her lover in the gloom
Of forest far—and thus her doom
Was life and joy—and motherhood—
Around her: smiles, a laughing brood!
I piped of love, that knew
No love—that was as new
To me, as is the pond to goose,
When from its mother's wings let loose.
I piped in exultation wild,
Such springing in the heart of child,
Piped as the birds in junipers—
As breezes through high conifers—
Piped livelily, my blood as guide,
Till tunes on air's sweet rivers plied!
Oh! there I piped a song as free
As piper lone in Arcady!
And piped as lone and sad
As he of haunted Hamelin had!
Oh! there I piped as they
Who wend their even-way
With quips and quircks, and laughters,
And smiles and wiles from daughters—
Such that Hannah bore—
And fifes are sounding evermore,
And dancers lead the throng,

That dream their wreathèd heads to song.
And one is sadly weeping,
Behind the rout: she's keeping
Vigil for one not come—
Who's in his early tomb!

May I remember yet,
When bloomed the violet,
At the first shower of Spring,
All by the marveling
Of prattling fells and brooks—
Deep, deep in woodland nooks—
With fragrant breaths of flowers,
That waft through vernal showers!
May I remember how I strode
Upon the dusty, sun-glared road,
When breezes quelled their breath,
And all seemed lost in death!
Save the supreme lone stillness bore
Upon its brow the majesty
Of Him, who blesseth evermore
Grand Nature with a grandeur free:
That blooms in storms, in torridness—
In bleakest bale—and sore distress!
Oh! on that road I whistled gay,
For well—so well!—I knew the way
I was to go: o'er hedges yellow,
Passed ivied huts, where hounds low bellow;
Where flits, and skims the air, the swallow—

Songs of Spring.

Where blooms the egglet-leavèd sallow;
Passed gentle whispers of the pines—
'Neath whom some maid-obstructed window shines!
Passed haw-haws, where the jasmine blooms,
And hears the murmurs of the far-off booms
Of torrent-cascades; where the sheep and goats
Are nibbling lawns of freshest green;—
Passed orchards that have a thousand throats;
With not one fruit, yet dressed in glowing sheen;
Where muttering creeks bicker on;
Where cowslips peep along the shore,
And bluets thread a maze all o'er;
And stately basks the lily lone
Its sallow graceful head; then I leap
The brooklet's crystal—where oziers weep—
Nay, laugh to the near solitude
And to the distant glittering wood;
For mourning is unknown to Spring—
Oh! Spring is glee, and trillering!
Then passed the spruce, the cedar, pine—
And where the winter-leaves recline:
There I linger in the cool retreat,
Far from the dust and new-born heat!
Thus wandered I to where
The Spring's cool, fragrant air
Is purified by brook and trees;
By song, and hymn, and virgin breeze.
Oh! there I spent rare moments of delight,
In God's fair halls, all in His guarding Sight!

WHERE THE DRAGON-FLIES FEED UPON THE TALL WHITE LILIES . . . .

To Mine Ocarino.

And on a cliff, whose zone
Was bathed by bubbling waters,
I perched—with thee as friend, alone,
To listen to brooklet's saddest laughters!
Oh! then the murmurs wedded with thy song,
And carried it upon their gurgles along!
(How sad I seem to feel anow!)
We sang together—rememberest thou?—
With spirited youth-delight—
As though I were brown Pan's gay self—
(And thou a token of some elf)
Piping on his reed
Where the dragon-flies feed
Upon the tall wild lilies—
And soothing, sweeting Phillis
By hazel-groves sitteth, there to keep
Dream-watch o'er Pales' sheep!
As though I were bewitched by spell—
Wrought by the tune's unconscious swell—
Changed to the lurid-browèd Lurelie:
The brook to Rhine near Bingen's glee—
My cliff to heights of mythy crags—
Below the maelstrom, when it drags
Skiffs, men, to deep, deep graves—
Whom ne'er a tepid tear-drop laves!
There all thy songs of sudden would quiver,
Like rippling harps on haunted river!
So we piped, and saw the shadows
Leave the woods, trail o'er the meadows.

Saw the glitter of the leaves ascend
To where the falcons' voices blend
With the crest-enhancéd breeze's tune—
All, all in warmest-hearted June!
Heard the silver knells,
Heard the chiming bells.
Heard the quaintness in the air—
When the sun is no more there.
Heard the distant water-wheel
Slowly melt within the brooklet's reel!
Heard the wren his liquid warble mate
With all the dreariness of evening late!
Heard the veil folding shimmeringly—
Heard the elfins busk for gloomy glee!
Heard sandpipers plead for places—
Heard Eve whisper to Night's star-eyed graces.
Heard the goblins trail the spruce with redlocks;
Heard the many sprites low-talk of wedlocks!
Heard the showers of angels drop;
Heard the owl on some oaken-top!
Heard the mysteries low moan—
Heard the sibyls musing alone!
Heard Eve's majesty upbear
Her sceptered hand to spell the dusk-blown air!
And heard the late cicada shrill—
Back of the dusk-enshrouded hill.
Oh! heard the silence, heard the calm—
Heard the dead death, heard the balm—
Oh! heard what no existence had—
Heard all—for sound is there, in all things sad!

THE MARINERS THE FIFES OF GHOST-WINDS HEAR!

Page 113.

And doth thy worn, black mould
Bring back the night of old,
When, with a friend, who with me learned
What, ages past, men's thoughts discerned,
I plied the inlet to the lake,
Where night-songs were awake.
And there, where water-witches—
(Hid where the shallow water twitches
The reeds, and wallows low–and birches—
Where, lone, the night-owl perches)
Their spelling moans so drearly move
From gurgling billows to the silent grove
And marshland-jungle—there we strayed,
And I upon thy weirder wild-notes played,
And let the boat be drawn along,
As flowed the stream its undersong;
And haunted crooks we spelled;
For now thy shrill woe swelled;
As, on some night of fret and fear,
The mariners the fifes of ghost-winds hear!
We saw the fairies, with their reytes
Drawn, tangling, through their glittering braids,
And heard their ouphen-rites slow rise
Up towards the vision-floating skies!
And now the pale, huge phantoms floated—
Then parted—high between, the gold-moon gloated,
And rimmed the shrouds with breath,
Such wafted from a pale-gold jasmine-wreath,
       An hour after death!

And, on the sallow-tingèd blue, a star
Twinkled—and seemed to glow; and, far
Around, the straying jewels of dream-Night
Wandered in their ever-wonted flight!
Then through the star-sprent liquid gloom
Thy love-tones glided, as a sail of doom,
Round whose dim ghastly glare there sound
The fancy-moans of the profound.
Or, as the sightless souls that cut their way
Through fires, to that sweet, pure, and deathless
    day!
Then with the symphony
Striking from Eternity
Its modulations to our earth,
(That hath at night its birth!)
The wavering wavelets wailed;
While to the wide, dark lake we sailed—
Passed one flare-beacon pale,
That telleth many a tale
Of wreck, disaster, plaints, and sighs—
And stranger, dark calamities—
All done when the moon was away:
A cry—a splash—silence—at home dismay!
And o'er the lake we shot!
Spelled wild, by mounts in distance gleaming;
And far through groves, the lone lights beaming!
While languorous fragrance wafted here—
Blown from the eve's so heavy-flowered bier!
And murmurs heard we far, far off;

And near, a whipping-sound, like water-demon's
  scoff!
Above, we seemed to see the angels hover
All seemed up there as calm, as weal of lover.
And o'er the lake we shot!
Tranced madly, by deeming night
Best tryst for visionary sight;
And, lured by some Syren-lays,
That wantoned o'er the rippled ways,
Our oars they foamed the gleaming waves;
As when wild Boreas raves
On snow-capped Titicaca's bosom,
To froth its flow to one snow-blossom!
We followed the lonely singing
To us such angel-senses bringing—
We passed them swiftly—maiden's they
Voicing sweet and clear some beauty lay.
As o'er the higher seas of musing
There oft meander songs, whose loosing
Is pain! so sang they, sweetly, clear,
As if the blessed alone should hear;
They sang, as once the swan-maids sang,
On fabled seas, where emeralds flowed—
And near, those silver-voices rang
That all the sea and heavens glowed!
Then rang their strains like plaintive sighs,
When some pure lily-blossom dies!
Their chanting seemed to stray away
As fumes that scent a funeral day:

Such that some honored nun received
When e'en the aspens and the flowers grieved!
Their sad, sweet swaying glided o'er,
As, passed some castled cliff so hoar,
(When proud Attila awed the world—
And war, and carnage, cursing swirled)
There floated, at the moon's uprise,
A craft where slow the river plies
O'er deepened bed,—and sorrow seems
Upwelling from the haunted gleams
Of the craft's wake; and mourning wails—
And sterner songs heave—and ascend
To where the eagle sails—
And departed thoughts in mystery wend
Their silent way! As down the river
Where rushes, lilies, and blossoms quiver,
There surges slow and faint
A voice, in soft love-plaint,
(One doomèd soul—in bane,
That joyed—instead to bear life's pain!)
That waileth plaintively,
As though it longèd not to be—
But longing in its wail,
It waileth, as the mid-stars wail—
So sang those voices, virgin-throated
While adown the sallow moon-eyes gloated!
Oh! on the night-breeze wafted
Those sweet songs of the fairy-crafted.
And as the night-breeze died,

To Mine Ocarino.

So all their languid singing sighed.
And with the night-moan's swelling
Their passion-dreams were welling,
Till, by the Nereids fondly borne, and tossed,
Their singing fainted—and was lost!
Then showered yet their echoes, lingering,
Like silent raining in the spring,
Where orange-blossoms, almond-trees
Incense the flower-freighted melodies!
And could thy note not stay
Their Syren-lay!
But no! my friend—no instrument
The world knows of, however blent
With Æolian softness, doth outweigh
The dulcet voice of maiden sweet!
Oh! listening to a girl-sung lay
How all our actions grow so fleet,
New worlds beam forth—it thrills our heart,
How can we from such witchery part!
O Ocarino, so we were friends
In boyhood's dreamy, drowsy days,
And now—no love-lip o'er me bends,
How can I pipe thy joyous lays!
   ITHACA, N. Y., 1885.

A SONG.

IT is the burden of a song
   That will not quit this longing soul—
 A song, when days were warm and long,
 I sang in answer to the oriole!
When o'er the fragrant path a maiden skipped,
 As blithely as gay Eos o'er the East!
I lured her to my tune, till she had lipped
 Of the quaint burden, and was pleased!

   It is the burden of a song
    That ever haunts my bleeding heart;
   A song, when frosty eves their throng
    Of dreamy vapors spun, called up a start
Within my breast to tell she wept alone—
 While to the sighing poplars, to the cave
That dwelled the wind, I sang in undertone,
 As through the night-storm the curled wave!

   It is the burden of a song
    That will not quit this longing soul—
   A song, when days were warm and long,
    I sang, in answer to the oriole!
When o'er the holts I chased a phantom-love—
 My maiden was a Dryad by the pool—

FOR CLOUDS WERE HANGING O'ER THE SKY.

When I had mused the skies by blossomed grove,
And had not known of Love's sad, grievous school!

LONG ISLAND, N. Y.

HOPE IS BORN OF CHANGE.

EIGHT days ago, I leaned against the window-sill,
   And gazed, with longing eyes, to yonder greening hill.
  Before the house, the apple-trees
    Were blooming fresh, and blossoming white.
  A vernal, soft, waylaying breeze
    Blew incense to me, as at balmy night;
Sweet carolling birds fluttered above the sun-bright eaves;
I felt, as though an angel whispered through the leaves
    Of the virescent apple-tree
    A faint sweet lay of prophesy!

To-day I gazed upon the scene, but with an eye
Of altered look, for clouds were hanging o'er the sky—

The blossoms lay scattered on the sod;
　　The apple-trees were green and gray;
　　A chilly wind, from Norland, plod
　　　His cheerless path o'er wolds of May!
Faint whistles from the outcast birds were the noon's lay,
And all my soul, with olden memories, seemed to say:
"Oh! Hope, wherever she may range,
　　Is wandering Child of Mother Change!"
ITHACA, N. Y.

SPRING-MORNING RHAPSODY.

THE white-flowered broom
　　Is now in bloom;
　　Four petals, snowy white,
Peep forth in Spring's delight!
The chaste green leaflets laugh
In Spring's behalf—
For, near the roots, gold flowers
Develop, by Spring's powers;
And, where the earth is seen,
Snow-flowers smile in between!

Spring-Morning Rhapsody.

The twitter of the merl,
And many a lyric purl
From twenty songsters in the trees,
   Proclaim that Hylas roams,
And sits, in silent groves, at ease,
   While creation foams!
Foams!--Delection is bursting,
Dead woods are fiercely thirsting
To sprout, and bloom the scene
With colors gay, and fresh light-green!
Who write the ecstasy
Of Spring's bright glee!
A man of noble mind
Can feel it when behind
The forehead Angel-bliss
Rings cheery, with Heaven's kiss!
But no agnostic head
Can know Spring's airy tread!
It needeth God-love so to feel
How Spring doth dance her madcap reel!
It must be true love's test
To *hear* Spring's fragrant zest!
O God! when lost in Thee,
So is Spring's melody!
And when I dream on Heaven,
So is to Spring sweet budding given!
And though no one believes
How sad my heart, how it grieves--
O God! when to the vernal woods
I go, what myriad marvel-moods

Of hero, Angel, God-head, crowd
In me, to make me proud—
Oh! proud that I may know
What Spring tells in her glow;
What all the flowers say
When they are in array!
What violets, and snow-star-flowers
Do whisper during vernal hours!
What in the vaporous air
Sings tepidly: Spring's there!

The cherry-trees are blushing;
Ground-flowers are fast pushing
   Their frail stems through the loam;
While sheep o'er gold-embossèd swards,
   So green and shining, roam—
All, all fair Spring's own fond awards!
Already bees are seen
Around the bushes green,
Whose buds are yet unblown;
But they have smelled the scent,
So linger: avid, bent
To have the first sip all alone!
The throstle trillereth,
Deriding paly Death!
And, through the coppice, flit
The phoebe, wren, and tit!
The fair box-elder sheds
His many tassels now—
While on the oaken bough

The squirrel merrily treads;
  And on the slanting lane
The robin hops and sings,
  While, drear, the phoebe-strain
A note from sorrow brings!

Oh! who can well enjoy
Spring's happiness—and cloy
His thoughts with growth's wild rapture!
He must Heaven's glow recapture.
No bliss on earth is like the one
When sharing it with Spring alone!
The man of noble mind
Can Spring-joy often find
When he doth feel Heaven's bliss
Conjoinèd with God's kiss!
But no one else—*for Spring
Is God's delicious marveling!*
Oh! who has ears, and eyes,
He contemplate Spring's skies;
And woods, and lakes, and flowers—
He cloy himself, some musing hours,
With Spring's ecstatic mood—
So it lead him to doing good!
The rippling triller-triller-chirp—
  The shrilly songs
That cicada-strains usurp—
  They shout: that Spring belongs
To Youth, and Joy—to goodly minds,
Such one in Virtue's region finds!

For Spring laughs at the cherry—
All bushes now are merry;—
And, by the lake, the broom
Has all its flowers in bloom!

CENTRAL PARK, 1890.

THE WHITE VIOLET.

O SHEENY, white violet!
   The stony brooklet's pet,
In it, like a diamond, set.

'Midst stones with moss o'ergrown,
In limp confusion thrown,
Thou fairest art alone!

O pale, meek violet,
Thy heart-leaves, dewy wet—
In them, like a jewel, set!

ADIRONDACKS, 1884,

THE STONY BROOKLET'S PET—

EVENING-STRAIN!

IT is a heavenly evening, golden and red—
And I, in anguish, trace back my short life's
    thread!
A haze hides dimly the bright hill,
Gay swallows fill
With song and motion all the fragrant air.
Behind the curtain-mist a sight of rare
Faint splendor plays with silken mien—
And magnified is all the scene:
Pine-trees stand out in bold outline,
Green meads, that slope, like smaragds shine;
Small houses display their simple thatches,
Sweet flowers are sparkling, grouped in patches.
O'er knolls, soft-draped in gauzy silk,
The sky takes hue of pinkish milk
And, blushing, beckons to the sun
To hurry on his weary run!

   * * * * *

On such an evening, flaming so,
I let my heart forget its woe;
To fondle a rare, celestial flower:
Great bliss for but a shortened hour!
No maid sublime, with raven hair or brow,
To me need then present her ardent vow,

My maid is fondest Nature fair,
Her smile thrills me—I stare! . . .
And drink her nectar, till I'm lost . . .
I see a motley host
Of Seraphs bask athwart the hill aglow—
Each one a smile of heavenly weal doth show!
Each halo to me brighter seems,
As God through all the faces gleams!
I wonder—and wonder—
A roar of thunder
Breaks all the saintly vision—
A May's rare spell to show me sights elysian!
1883.

THE BLACKBIRD.

WHAT black thing is flying through the trees,
 While the azure sky with brightning spring
   Is triumphing.
Warmer grow the vernal melodies,
While upon a branch of budding birches
   The blackbird perches.

Oh! what change upon its feathers black—
Sure, sun's magic vies with vernal flowers
   And summer-showers!

The Blackbird.

As the sun-rays bathe the bird's fair back
All the jewels of the splendorous East
                On neck, wing, breast,

Glow and glitter, dance and sparkle and sheen:
Smaragdine on neck—dark lazuli-hue
                Its breast doth imbue;
Wings of ebon turn to rarest green,
Mixed with schorly topaz, jasper tint,
                All without stint!

Blackbird—so ill-named by folk and boor—
Thee a poet saw this glorious morn
                When jewels adorn
Thy feathers, like sparkles on a Kohinoor!
God His marvel shows: His fair work glows
                In all that grows!
   CENTRAL PARK, 1892.

THE SMELL OF SHADE.

THE smell of shade
   In new May's mellow glade!
   The grace of leafèd trees in green—
The smiling blooms of bushes in between,
Where sparkling sun-rays skip and flow—
There, soul and I may go!

The smell of shade
The May-hours doth pervade—
The lilacs low spend rare perfume;
The dandelions the nooks illume
With golden glow, or balls of light;
While soul and I are bright!

The smell of shade
Ah me! where bare brakes dreary made
The fallow lawn or rolling hills,
The dream of May each air-nook fills;
All laughs in green and jewel-hues—
My soul and I imbues!

The smell of shade!
Through succulent tall thick grass we wade,
All under groves of dense-leaved trees—
Dog-wood, pink hawthorn, bird-berries,

The Smell of Shade.

Bloom radiant in May's air so sweet—
For both of us so meet!

The smell of shade
Intoxicates each young grass-blade;
The silver trees, snow-draped, exhale
Their subtle perfumes rare and pale—
Visterias and catalpas bloom—
Sweet memories for our room!

The smell of shade!
How can life's glorious love-fire fade,
When all is blooming in the woods,
And scents bring magic to man's moods—
May-songs enliven all the scene,
Could woe have ever been?

The smell of shade
In new May's sumptuous glade!
The rich wet green of trees and lawn;
O'er all a veil of perfumes drawn,
So thick—the shade exhales a scent,
With thee and me 'tis blent!

The smell of shade—
The lute-fall, where the lilacs fade—
The warbles through the flowering groves,
All sing to May about their loves,
Their feelings by the bubbling dale—
We know them rich and hale!

The smells of shade,
Where bushes laugh—the air pervade.
With scents from blossoms of all hues!
May thus fair nature's world imbues—
By lawn, in woods, and valley's glow;—
There, soul! we both may go!

CENTRAL PARK, 1892.

MAY 4TH, 1891.

THERE is a fluent, fitful breeze that blows
    Below the glowing sun—
While virgin May mellifluous gifts bestows
    On every happy one.

Not from the briny deep air-sprites have brought
    The liquid, that thrills this noon;
But all the joyous wanton air is fraught
    With crystal waters boon.

As though May spelled the thousand springs
    Of all our mountain-sides
To rise—and shed around their murmurings,
    So freshest joy abides.

There is a liquid flow of breezy air
    From mount-pools fresh upsprung;
While virgin-May lets flow her flowery hair
    Around or old or young!

PAIN AFTER DREAMS.

THOU sun! didst flatter with thy rays the skies,
    This morning early, when the cocks did crow!
    Rain's jewels hung upon the maple-row,
And sparkled where the lessening wind-breath
        sighs;
Too on the distant hill sweet prophesies
    Of clear air rose—did melt within the glow
    Of thy supremest light! the hum, so low,
Of trudging bees foretold a warm surprise!

But when Aurora fled the crowding hours,
    The hoppers of the fields no longer chirred—
    Huge, swollen clouds of rain o'erhead demurred—
        While no more flies danced in thy living
            beams—
And drear again grew all the glistening bowers—
    Alas! so comes a pain aft' brightest dreams!
LAKEWOOD, N. J.

SPRING'S FACILITY TO SING.

I FEEL it come—as April feels the Spring
   With rosy growths and ruby-blooms return—
   That song-thrill that in all my soul doth burn,
Even like the soft-flaméd marveling
That keeps so mellow all songs, May-birds sing;—
   I feel it creep—not asp-wise 'neath a fern,
   But even as steaming heat, when violets yearn
To bud, creeps o'er Spring-leas, o'er everything!

I feel the flower-ease to sprout and blossom—
   The sweet delicious abandon o' the bee
   That, without work, doth sip June's honey free—
Oh! as pink roses, top of virgin's bosom,
   Fast cluster at a faint tune love doth say—
   So easily will come my rich sweet lay!

THE WILDERNESS OF MUSIC.

OH, let those lulling strains that sing of love,
    And are so vaporous to live unseen,
    Float my mind's labyrinthine halls atween,
Like sacred alleys in Dodona's grove—
Where man's own fate was ruled by dove and dove!
    And let them linger like sweet scents—or sheen
    Of sun—till they mature to dreams so green
As once were dreamed by Juno-loving Jove!

Amphion's shell ne'er moved the wooded hills,
    Or glistening stones, as thy tune moves me now.
    I loose birth, death—but on oblivion's bough
I lean, and feel the breath of asphodels
    That bathes me quite—and thou dost seem to be
    A nebulous song whose life is meant for me!

SING AGAIN.

O BARGE of my wild genius, quick unfurl
   Thy sails, for we must sail o'er ocean's blue
   To yonder beach, where grow the palm and yew.
There while away the time, by shell and pearl—
Mayhap be soothed by some fair Nereid girl,
   Who singeth to the sea-lay tunes so true
   That fill our souls, to sing sweet melodies too,
Sweet as her voice, yet wild as ocean's swirl!

It is because these long last days no tone
   Came forth from my good genius's lyre.
   So reef thy sails, and do as I desire:
To take us to those shores, fair Musing's own,
   Where we may rest, and sing of Homer dead;
   Of those great souls who all the world have led!

IMPROMPTU.

LOS ANGELES' SPRING.

O LET me go
  Where all the lisping willows blow;
  Where they their chestnut-budlings show—
Bursting, with eyes of silken snow.
Where, near the reeds, the runnels flow;
And flowers golden in gay families grow!
      There let me go
When willows all their snow-eyed budlings show!

      Then let me hear
The yellow-breasted birdling, singing near,
His song so clear with sun and cheer;
And listen to the low sounds in the mere
Where blood-red weeds trail, as in fear,
With the runnel's gush, that knows no singing drear;
      There let me hear
The sounds of nature, singing: sun and cheer!

      Then let me see
The hills roll in each other beauteously,
And clumps of trees dream on them free .—
On willow-catkins, how the gold-thighed bee

Buzzes, then sips them, in security.
And too, the golden fruited orange-tree,
      Such let me see
While blue skies shine, and blows the breeze so free.

MAY THE FIRST.

IS this the first of May!—in town still pent!
  Not hearkening to the starling in the brake;
  Nor seeing anemones by stilly lake;
Nor, pensive, walking, where the white fawn went
To lip the saffron pool at noon's advent.
    Ah me! 'tis stale convention chains me still
    To stony streets; far from the vocal hill,
Away from dimpling dales, fuming with scent!

Oh! Shelley—nay, my Keats, or thou
  Who didst rare daisies weave for "Charitie"—
  Would ye have so forsworn May's minstrelsy;
Oblivious of the gemmèd apple-bough,
    Enjoying but in mind: the sweets of May;
    The jubilee of Spring's most fragrant day?

AWAY FROM DIMPLING DALES . . . . .
Page 136.

THIS CAME TO ME.

OH! art thou in some verdurous valley hiding,
    Low in some nook—lost, pensive and alone;
    While languidly the noon-sun pours upon
The sleeping snake that ever is abiding
Near to that grot, o'er whom the russet-golden
    Broad-spreading beech in girly Spring's in leaf—
    There dreaming on thy days that bore a grief
To thee—evoking loves of moments olden?

Low in the lulling murmur of those leaves,
    That in the May have colors of the fall;
    While all the valley's growths, or large or small,
    In vernant tremors ripple tales to thee—
Oh! art thou far from hospitable eaves—
    Alone, by verdant Spring—away from me?

NO END.

OH! I can never end my life of song;
    How can the mavis cease his madcap trill—
    How can the ripples on the April-rill
Curtail their gladdening singing all day long!
Or who would wish the lark would no more throng
    The morning with his gay songs—how they thrill!
    How can the rapturous nightingales be still—
Only when death strikes them—and doeth wrong!

But me no death can take away—my singing
    Is antepast of the fair joyous Heaven;
    Anticipate with me, who am so driven
To sing and sing—the jubilant angel-ringing,
    When souls of God will be in realms serene
    Some day—when what we sang the world will
        glean!

NEW BLOOMS.

THE heat of yesterday hath yielded more
    Than many days of temperate weather give—
    For now the yellow dandelions live,
Studding with gold-balls hillside, and the shore
That mellows the low laughter of new-come birds.
    The shrubs are verdant-budding; and the trees
    Show myriad eyes, red sprouts, or panoplies
Of tassels—designed to shade the summer-herds.

What gladness irradiates from the teeming earth!
    Smiles, dimples, laughter, love-notes, nodding heads!
    Blushing in wantoness, Spring gladness sheds—
All mimic, in their joy, the maiden Mirth,
    And, lost to dolor, children of Happiness
    Bound forth from every fold of Spring's sweet dress!

CONTENTMENT.

I GLORY when my seven senses are
   Content; for then I *feel* the warm sun lave
  My health-sworn body, as with tepid wave.
I *taste* the sweet salubrious air, that far
Doth move with tempered breezes; near, doth float
   About me like perfume from censers rare.
  I *see* the eucalyptus-trees be shaken where
The hill-top slopes to dales; I *hear* the note

From bird; the silken strain of pleasing wind.
  I *smell* the scents from grasses on the hill.
I *dream* here, for sweet nature is so kind
   To let my heart and soul be calm and still.
And last, though not in church where myths are told,
With God of all I do communion hold!
  Los Angeles, South Cal.

THREE SPRINGS IN ONE WEEK.

O HAVE my feet trod Sicily's sweet flowers
   While o'er them trembled Spring's lithe fairies
     all—
I've seen the blue, quiet sea; the orange-bowers;
   Date-trees in fruit; and the proud palm-tree
     tall.
Then, through chill Italy, to Venice fair—
   Where winter no consent yet gave to bud
The almond—nor the lemon; then, down there
   Where Doria is as Cæsar in the flood
Of common parlance, Genoa proud—ay, proud
   With countless palaces, on dreamy hills appeared.
Then, 'long the rich Riviera—where Spring's cloud
   Had showered prodigal—to Nice!—so cheered
Me three strange Springs in one fair week's short
     time;
I've relished Spring thrice—each in other clime!
NICE, FRANCE, 1887.

THE POET.

IN MEMORY OF THE LATE FRANCIS S. SALTUS.

A WISE magician, he is as the air,
    That cold, can make the mountain-waters cease
To flow;—when warm, can winter-plains release
From cruel frost—and make the woodlands fair,
With gold-green leaves, and flowers; birds singing there!
    He's as the miracle of sweet increase:
    Where one tree stood—aft' years of warmth and peace,
A forest spreads, rich-grown with flowers rare!

One wood-brook bubble shows him fair Fatme's founts;
    One tear seen, blossoms in him worlds of stories;
    Inspired, he dreams o'er Fancy's promontories—
Sees fair vast lands, heaven's blue, and seas, and mounts—
    And, like the sun, that months with flowers doth dress—
    So he bewitches all to loveliness!

NATURE IS NEVER THE SAME.

THE day is gone—the heat o' the distant sun,
  Whose fire-wheels turn ceaselessly, is cool;
The champing steeds have left their stalls, to run
Through scented grass to some lone dimpled pool!
The crickets chirr no more—and stillness breathes,
While light still lives; and Luna smiles, and wreathes
Her silvery chaplet 'round the quiet earth!
The day is gone—but, in its stead, the West
Lays scarlet on, that, gradual, turns to gold—
And in the beechen grove new songs have birth:
The whip-poor-wills are frantic in Eve's rest;
While 'thwart the glare the bats wheel round some fold!
The day is gone—but, in the solemn calm,
The moon looks down—and nature sings a psalm!
  LAKEWOOD, N. J.

TO THE MEADOW-LARK.

HAST thy fresh and liquid song
    From young Aegle's throat—
  Singing all the bright day long
    Sweetest sparkling note:
Clear and fresh as large drops falling down
On the surface of the brook-pool brown?

  Oh! such crystal prelude low,
    Ere thy gurgle falls
  On the air, with sun aglow,
    To me ever calls
Up some memory in that vernal grove:
Where the stream's purl was my only love!

  Art thou on the rose-grown fence,
    Whistling to the knolls;
  As an only recompense
    An echo far, that rolls
Over yon green hillock—to the bay:
Hillock flowery—where the snow-gulls stay!

  Nay, thy mate doth answer thee.
    There she flieth fleet
  To the bough o' yon hawthorn-tree:
    Where you both will meet

To the Meadow-Lark.

In a moment: gurgling out your love—
True as lovers' own in elder-grove.

    Stay awhile near th' meadow green,
      Scented from fair flowers;
    Radiant, in the Spring's bright sheen,
      As those fragrant bowers
Hafiz sat in, listening to the tale
Of his Morning's joyful nightingale!

    Melody moves sweetly on
      Through a scented air—
    Thine is but a sweet flute-tone
      With a gurgle clear—
Yet in it the spirit of a ripple dwells—
Such that, in bright woods, the maid-fawn spells.

    Joyous must thy spirit be;
      Fresh as mountain-spring!
    Givest thou thy mood to me
      When in woods I sing:
Sing of mosses, whispering trees, and lakes—
Till my strain the slumbering world awakes?

    So thou dost my dreams inspire!
      Meadow-lark! Call—call—
    Till the air is filled wi' desire
      To be thy fondest thrall!
Then I feel thy song upon my cheek—
I hearken—forgetting how to see or speak!

Then all vanishes: this broil
   'Tween pelf-men, and those
Deeming all our life a toil;
   All our cares, our woes;
And the curse that souls must earn their way,
Spite of showing on their brows Heaven's Lay!

This world's sin, and low delight—
   Poverty and wrong—
Turn to visions, cool and bright—
   Hearkening to thy song.
Would thou couldst thy magic use to beam
Love again—impearl on life Love's dream.

Under the Eucalyptus-tree
   Listening to thy purl,
What doth it recall to me;
   Trill'ring of a girl:
Lying on a meadow, gold and white;
Or the ghost of some dissolved Delight!

More like sounds in euchlore-wolds,
   Where snow-violets muse.
More like drops in fairy-folds,
   Where, from grottoes, ooze
Mossy waters;—more like sprinkling showers
On a quiet pool, by Pan's deep bowers.

More like tinklings of the pods
   On the acacia boughs—

To the Meadow-Lark.

Far on Syria's sheeny sods—
　　When Harmattan blows;
More like dancing bubbles down a fall—
More like bells at rites fantastical.

　　Gurgle away, thou happy bird!
　　　　Knowing not one care—
　　Feeling never longing's gird—
　　　　Ever—ever fair
Thy nest, thy flying-realm; thy life—
Oh! where love, and song, and dreams are rife!

　　Art thou on the rose-grown fence—
　　　　Thou with breast of gold,
　　Star-flower-radiant—as a recompense
　　　　An echo—from the fold
Where the kine and steeds are grazing—where
Bluetts, cranebills, marigolds are fair!

　　Nay, thou hast thy mate! to show
　　　　Thee rare cheerfulness;
　　She percheth by the apple-row—
　　　　Listeneth to the stress
Of thy flute-like whistle, wi' that gurgle clear—
See! she flieth—resteth all so near!

　　Stay awhile by yon green wood,
　　　　Fragrant with Spring-flowers;
　　Fill with song my solitude—
　　　　Many, many hours—

Many years—so that, on weary days,
Thy flute-note be key to my joy-lays!

    Three bell-notes from heaven come;
      Rippling laughter then.
    Like sweet whistling, where roses bloom
      In some vernal glen.
Meadow-lark! thy call is dear to me—
Brings bright days of joyous infancy!

    Hast thy song from Aegle's throat
      Meadow-lark! say, say!
    That sweet gurgle, that flute-like note
      Have such magic sway:
That I would to lie on flowers of Spring,
Rapt, nepenthe-bathed, to hear thee sing!
SAN RAFAEL, SOUTH CALIFORNIA, 1889.

RHAPSODIA.

RARE dowager of Spring, eternal sun!
    Thou comest here again
      To fill with fragrance all the plain.
        The woods and hillsides low
        Where limpid brooklets flow—
      And flowers that colored glow—

Rhapsodia.

As varied as an Ouled's dress-magnificence
When she doth her quaint dances slowly dance.
    And through the air
    The birds more sweetly sing and pair,
The frolicking roebucks play and run—
While life renewed lives now in everyone!

Last night the fishes in the skies
    Would sport in their own spheres;
    For drops fell down to fill the meres
      And drench the plants and trees;
      And soak the earth, the breeze.
    Yet would the rain not cease.
But fell and fell with tinkle and with moan—
That sorrow crept to him who was alone.
    And through the night
    Lost was the owl's lone delight.
All went to sleep with dreary eyes—
A dirge on every lip—and tears and cries!

But thou eternal sun! this morn hast come
    Again to sing thy glory
    Athwart the hill and promontory—
      To fill the hearts of all
      With joy so magical;
      That to rare song a thrall
Was every throat—as in the world's beginning
The stars sang strains unknown to woe or sinning!

  And through the morn
  A bright new song of life was born—
That shed upon the sad, sad tomb
  A light—and made of all our woe a bloom!
BISKRA, ALGERIA, AFRICA, DEC., 1892.

AN INSPIRATION.

O PINES, in clusters standing,
  Ye shed a quiet solemn gloom—
 While Spring, with soft commanding,
Bids nature burst with bud and bloom.

Sacred your groves, endarkened
  By the weird green, embowering all—
In days of old, kings hearkened
  To voices in your awing hall.

Now, only birds are singing;
  And winds through ye enhance their song—
For all our race is clinging
  To Mammon cold—who breeds great wrong.

But yet a poet's dreaming
  Finds in your gloom a solemn tone:
Which, in the future's gleaming,
  Will richly roll, when I am gone!
CENTRAL PARK, NEW YORK CITY, 1892.

RAIN OF SPRING.

VERNAL rains are falling—
Liquid strains are calling
All the fairies hither—
To fill the roses' cups
So they will not wither,
But be sweet when Hylas sups;—
To drench the musk-rose leaf,
That its efflorescence-
Time be lightning-brief;
To cloy the erubescence
Of the almond-buds with blood,
Such that thrills sweet Naidhood!
Vernal rains are streaming;
While the mounts are steaming!
All the fields with flowers
Pray to Spring's fresh showers,
As a virgin prays
When her lover delays!
While the birds are singing—
Sweetest sounds are ringing
By the swollen brooks—
Near fair, hidden nooks;
Where are star-flower-beds—
Mab dreamwise o'er mosses treads.

And the gentle rain
Hath its own sweet strain:
Dream-seas sing not so—
Nor the undersong of woe
Dulcet pain to sound transposes
As Spring-rain on buds of roses!

NICE, FRANCE, 1887.

IL PRIMO di MAGGIO.

LONTAN' è il invierno negro—
   Entraa noi il spiro allegro
      Del' primavera!
Partito la fria essenza—
Bisbiglia il rio en cadenza.
      In nostra spera
Tutto parla un' lieto linguaggio—
Perchè oggi è il primo di Maggio!

Ah! canta l'ucello
Suo canzonello
      Con' allegrezza—
Il fiore purpureo
Rid' a su' iddèo
      Com' un' altezza
Del Sud a' su seniore selvaggio—
Perché oggi è il primo di Maggio!

SBALZA LA CAPRICUOLA.

Page 153.

Il Primo di Maggio.

Sopra la zolla
Com' un' festiva folla
    La erba surge.
Nel' bosco fiorito
Il zimbellito
    Col' stagione turge.
E piu caldo è del sol il raggio—
Perchè oggi è il primo di Maggio!

Ah! vien' a biacciarmi—
Col' alma amarmi—
    Donzella bella!
Sbalza la capricuola—
Canta la rusignuola
    La sua favella—
Perché gli arboli a oltraggio
Brillan' nel' sue veste di Maggio!

Tu' treccie di capelli
Ondeggiano, com' velli
    Nel' aria greca—
Tu sorriso riflette
Le giovane rossette—
    Lontan' de la zecca;—
E tuoi occhi, com' è tu' usaggio,
Parlan' la gioia del' primo di Maggio.

Ta voce trabocca
E, presso del' rocca,

Tuoi accenti
Mischiano in petto
Col' riveletto
E raggii ardenti—
E mi piace piu ch' en un palagio—
Perchè tu canti al' primo di Maggio!

Io, garzonotto,
En amor' son' dotto—
Mi' gavazza cola
Nel' aria lieta—
O sensa meta—
E, mia Sola!
Tu' baccio è com' il messaggio
Divino che fa fiorir' il Maggio.

Lontan è il invierno negro—
Entra a noi il spiro allegro
Del' primavera—
Partito la fria essenza—
Bisbiglia il rio en cadenza!
In nostra spera
Tutto parla un lieto linguaggio—
Perchè oggi è il primo di Maggio!

1894.

UNO QUESITO.

" ISOLE Fortunate!
　"Dove siete?"
　Rispondemmi una Fantasma:
"Nel' immaginazione
"Dell' anima humana!"

"Dov' posso trovare
　"Arie liete,
"Per sempre cantare,
　"Com' l'ucello nel' bosco?"

"Ningun' luogo esiste
　"Fanciullo mio!
"Songe al' sole triste,
　"Allora sarai
"Com' un Angelo benito!"

"Songe, songe—sempre!
　"Fino Il Dio
"Te dare espressione
　"Per cantar' e cantare—
"Della vita divina!"

"Isole Fortunate!
　Dove siete?"

Rispondemmi un Angelo:
" Nel' immaginazione
" Dell' anima humana!"

Cantero per sempre
   Delle isole,
Pieno de venture—
   Pieno delle songe
Che hanno gli ucelli lieti!

"Canta, fanciullo mio!
   "Pure parole—
"Per viaggiar' ai luoghi
   " Dov' son le Isole Fortunate!"

ENVOI.

LOVE! laugh not at these self-taught songs—
  I know they bring no treasures rare;
But would the world be proud and great,
If gold or jewels or nature's state—
And all that to wealth's show belongs—
  Were not upon this globe so fair?

Trade could not be—if earth
  Were barren as the desert sands.
    Wealth could not live if rare gold fail.
    Proud man is thankless—the many rail
At those who give to song sweet birth—
  And pelf is honored in all lands.

Love! this is true—but with no flowers—
  No summer's fruits—no mountain's ore—
    Trade, show, nor wealth could be ashine—
    So in the mind or soul divine
No pleasures live, if through life's hours
  None sing or praise from heart's deep core!

FINIS.

ERRATA.

Page 37; tenth line read *passing* for sing.
Page 66; last line read *nor* for or.
Page 71; fifth line from below read *Who* for that.
Page 71; last lines read *cheeks*, *speaks* for cheek, speak.
Page 92; first and second stanza read *even as* for as even.
Page 90; last stanza read *rose* for twined.
Page 103; thirteenth line read *boozy* for boozed.
Page 105; tenth line read *with* for in.
Page 152; tenth line read *Entra a* for Entraa.

www.ingramcontent.com/pod-product-compliance
Lightning Source LLC
Chambersburg PA
CBHW032228230426
43666CB00033B/1637